THE MYTH OF
THE GOLDEN YEARS

*A Socio-Environmental
Theory of Aging*

THE MYTH OF
THE GOLDEN YEARS

A Socio-Environmental
Theory of Aging

By

JABER F. GUBRIUM

Assistant Professor of Sociology
Department of Sociology and Anthropology
Marquette University

With a Foreword by

David O. Moberg

Professor of Sociology
Department of Sociology and Anthropology
Marquette University

CHARLES C THOMAS · PUBLISHER
Springfield · Illinois · U.S.A.

Published and Distributed Throughout the World by
CHARLES C THOMAS • PUBLISHER
Bannerstone House
301-327 East Lawrence Avenue, Springfield, Illinois, U.S.A.

© 1973, by CHARLES C THOMAS • PUBLISHER
ISBN 0-398-02703-X (Cloth)
ISBN 0-398-02757-9 (Paper)
Library of Congress Catalog Card Number: 72-88494

With THOMAS BOOKS *careful attention is given to all details of manufacturing and design. It is the Publisher's desire to present books that are satisfactory as to their physical qualities and artistic possibilities and appropriate for their particular use.* THOMAS BOOKS *will be true to those laws of quality that assure a good name and good will.*

Printed in the United States of America
W-2

For Suzanne

FOREWORD

DURING THE EARLY development of social gerontology the concept of "adjustment" became a major focus of attention in theory and research about aging. On the personal level it implies the necessity of adjusting, i.e. changing one's attitudes and behavior in order to adapt successfully to changes in his social situation, while social adjustment involves the adaptation of society or its normative standards, operating procedures, or institutions in such manner as to increase social efficiency and facilitate the personal adjustment of its members (Cavan et al., 1949:10-17).

Changes in the life situation of a person, such as illness, retirement, death of his or her spouse, unemployment, and moving to another residence, occur in the context of a society which also is in transition, one which imposes various demands, expectation, and pressures upon the individual. Thus the person who hypothetically is adjusted in middle age may become either stimulated or frustrated from entrance into a new situation as a result of personal and family changes or modifications in his social environment accompanying aging. This leads to unadjustment and restlessness or to aggressive reactions, which could result either in adjustive behavior or in maladjustment.

Maladjustment, in turn, is indicated by various forms of neurotic and psychotic reactions, including imaginary ailments, anxiety, guilt feelings, phobias, alcoholism, suicide, mental breakdowns etc., which replace or impede functional responses to crises. But as a result of reoriented attitudes, adaptation of activities to fit new circumstances, or both, readjustment is possible. To assist the elderly to readjust, it was felt that resources of the primary group and community, education for new activities, and therapeutic and counseling services should be made available (Cavan et al., 1949:14-17).

Out of the concern for personal and social adjustment emerged the "activity theory" which Professor Gubrium describes in his stimulating theoretical study. Providing suitable activities and then helping, educating, and enticing old persons into them was viewed as the best means for making old age "the golden years." Golden Age Clubs sprang up all over the nation; senior citizen centers were established in hundreds, if not thousands, of communities; churches organized special classes, circles, and societies for their older members and friends; the American Association of Retired Persons, with a wealth of activity opportunities, was founded and began its rapid growth. Activity was viewed as the path to good adjustment.

Both experience and research, however, made it apparent that activity was not always possible, nor did it invariably result in effective coping, as Gubrium indicates in Chapter I. Instead, it seemed, many people adjusted best when they capitulated to the realities of their situation and gradually withdrew from social involvements with their advancing age. The "disengagement theory" thus constituted another branch of the adjustment orientation to aging. Both society and the elderly were mutually involved in moving older people out of social responsibilities; the adjusted person was viewed as the one who adapted peacefully to his personal and social changes by mentally accepting the reality of his diminishing associations. But disengagement theory also has weaknesses and flaws for which it has been attacked from its very beginning.

Professor Gubrium has developed a new socio-environmental approach to aging to overcome the weaknesses of both the activity and disengagement theories. Since his book is in the reader's hands, there is no point in my presenting his resolution of the dilemmas created by the other approaches. Suffice it to say that his theory introduces a masterful blend of the strengths of both older theories while it overcomes their most serious weaknesses, inconsistencies, and inadequacies. It makes clear how strongly interrelated individual factors and the socio-cultural environment are in the attitudes and behavior of the aged (and by implication all other age-groups). It provides a solid basis for understanding both the elderly and the American cultural myth of the golden years in the sunset and twilight of life.

Although his language does not make it obvious, Gubrium's theory can nevertheless be located in the context of the enduring search for good personal and social adjustment for older people. How best to promote social conditions that facilitate their coping and foster morale, happiness, life satisfaction, contentment, peace of mind, fulfillment, comfort—in short, wholesome adjustment—for the aging and elderly is the implicit practical question that lurks beneath his theoretical analysis.

This book therefore will be of interest and help to social workers, medical doctors, family counselors, clergymen, nurses, attorneys, and others working in the applied areas of geriatrics as well as to gerontologists, sociologists, psychologists, and their students. The theory is here. What remains to be done is the lengthy, complex task of testing it and more fully developing its implications for society and for the elderly, those who work with them, and the younger generations whose lives are inextricably intertwined with those of the aged and who themselves are daily moving closer to the mythical "golden years" of life.

DAVID O. MOBERG

PREFACE

As an academic discipline, social gerontology is quite young—about three decades old. In this short time, two rather distinct perspectives on aging have emerged. One, sometimes labeled "activity theory," has focused on the individual efforts which aged persons make toward maintaining a satisfactory state of psychological well-being. The other, "disengagement theory," orients itself around varied dimensions of the social systems of which older people are a part, attending to the reciprocal influences between such systems and the process of aging, emphasizing an alleged gradual withdrawal of persons from social systems. The approach to aging taken here has affinities with both of the existing perspectives; it combines the emphasis on the individual resources of aged persons made by activity theorists with the potential interest of a disengagement theorist in the differential demands on persons of varied social environments.

There is an increasing need for constructing a new, more inclusive approach to the sociology of "normal" aging. Since the formulation of activity (forties) and disengagement (early sixties) theories, the accumulation of data on the process of aging has matured to a stage that eclipses either of their empirical scopes alone. This has made it difficult to account for variations in the process of aging that are due to "other significant factors" not handled well by either perspective singly. The parsimony of one general perspective rather than dual perspectives on the data of aging simplifies explanation and increases the explanatory capacity of our understanding of the process of growing old. Any propositions deduced from a more general approach have a wider empirical scope. The general point of view constructed here has been named the "socio-environmental approach" to aging.

Chapters I and II set the background for a discussion of

socio-environmentalism. Current theories of aging are focused upon in Chapter I, outlining the structure of the theories, their underlying assumptions about the behavior of old people and their explanatory problems. Chapter II introduces the socio-environmental approach to aging. First, some of the conceptual sources of socio-environmentalism are discussed. Second, the two empirical sources of the approach are delineated: (1) existing studies of aging that combine individual and environmental concepts, and (2) a 1969-70 study of the behavior of aged persons in varied kinds of social contexts in Detroit.

Much of the data examined in this book was generated from intensive interviews with and observations of 210 persons, aged sixty to ninety-four, in Detroit. This is referred to throughout the following chapters as the "Detroit Study." The main concern of the study was to explore the utility of combining individual and environmental concepts in understanding the behavior of aged persons.

Chapters III and IV delineate two components of the socio-environmental approach: social contexts and individual resources, respectively. In Chapter III a typology of age-relevant social contexts is constructed, with a systematic discussion of the kinds of problems for everyday life that each type is likely to pose for the aged. Chapter V turns to another component of the socio-environmental approach to aging. Here individual resources that affect behavior flexibility in old age are outlined. Depending on the degree of a person's flexibility, his behavior is either highly influenced by the contingencies of his social context or relatively oblivious to them.

In Chapter V the socio-environmental point of view is used to explore the relative influences of resources and social contexts on aged persons. The combination of resource and social contextual factors is considered in terms of the "limits" or constraints each places on aged persons' coping abilities. Hypotheses on the morale outcomes of various kinds of individual resource-social context congruency are proposed. The criminal victimization of the elderly is examined, and additional hypotheses about the impact of individual resources and social contexts on victimization and victimization beliefs are stipulated.

Chapter VI explores the effects of environmental age-concentration on the emergence of group-consciousness among old people. This is examined in terms of the stages of emerging group-consciousness and the factors that affect the development of consciousness from one stage to another.

In the last chapter, criticism is made of a variety of popular conceptions of old age labeled "the myth of the golden years." First, various dimensions of the myth are outlined with examples of images that appear in popular literature, the mass media, and advertisements. Second, a discussion of each of these dimensions follows from the viewpoint of socio-environmentalism together with relevant data on the behavior of aged persons.

Throughout this book, the socio-environmental approach to old age is utilized in examining other theories, existing data on the behavior of the elderly, and popular images of old age. In addition, however, an effort has been made to develop the critical capacity of the socio-environmental point of view. This critical capacity is implicitly a part of all theories. Here, it has been made explicit.

ACKNOWLEDGMENTS

THIS BOOK HAD ITS beginning in a research project that I conducted in Detroit in 1969-70, which explored the utility of combining environmental and individual concepts in analyzing the morale and life satisfaction of the aged. For her encouragement during the research as well as her insights, I wish to thank Professor Eleanor P. Wolf of the Department of Sociology at Wayne State University.

Also, I owe a debt of gratitude to my colleague and friend, Dr. David O. Moberg. He patiently and critically read the manuscript for logic and style. It has profited from his knowledge of the gerontological literature and his research experience in the field of aging.

Several persons were instrumental in facilitating various technical aspects of the Detroit Study. For this, I wish especially to thank my wife, Suzanne, for her help in programming and data processing, and Miss Pauline Brimhall of the Well-Being Service of Detroit for generously offering the use of her files and office space.

Finally, I want to acknowledge the clerical and typing assistance of Mrs. Sharron Johns.

JABER F. GUBRIUM

CONTENTS

THE MYTH OF
THE GOLDEN YEARS

A Socio-Environmental
Theory of Aging

Chapter I

CURRENT THEORIES OF AGING

THE SOCIOLOGY OF aging has been influenced by two distinct approaches to the social behavior of old people. These competing viewpoints usually have been referred to as "activity" and "disengagement" theories. The differences between them stem largely from the implicit assumption that each makes about the relationship between individual persons and collective behavior expectations. Although they are theoretically distinct, both have suffered severe explanatory problems methodologically, as well as empirically. Neither has been able to account for a significant number of documented instances of old people's behavior that contradict what might have been predicted from its viewpoint alone.

The focus of their arguments has been primarily the nature of the interrelationship between general activity or social interaction, on the one hand, and morale or life satisfaction, on the other. Activity and disengagement theorists have argued that particular types of activity or social interaction, respectively, in old age more readily lead to life satisfaction than others. Their arguments attempt to explain variations in life satisfaction resulting from overt behavioral differences among the aged. Neither has dealt extensively with the reverse possibility, namely, that persons characterized by specific types of morale or life satisfaction in various situations may actively approach and deal with their social worlds differently.

Compared to activity theory, the explicitness of the disengage-

3

ment approach is clear and distinct. This is probably a result of two factors. First, activity theory has never been definitely named as such, but rather is a label that has been attached to an implicit body of literature about activities and morale in old age. Second, disengagement theory emerged about ten years after the activity approach and was partially constructed as a conscious rebuttal to activity arguments (cf. Cumming & Henry, 1961, pp. 16-23).

ACTIVITY THEORY

As a sociological approach to aging, activity theory had its professional beginning with the publication of Cavan, Burgess, Havighurst, and Goldhammer's *Personal Adjustment in Old Age* (1949). Aging here is conceived primarily as a problem in the personal resolution of strains on self-conception resulting from changes in later life roles. Differentiation is made between two types of conceptions. On the one side, emphasis is placed on the social structural aspects of growing old in American Society:

> . . . relinquishment of social relationships and roles typical of adulthood, and acceptance of social relationships and roles typical of the later years but not of earlier adulthood (Cavan *et al.*, 1949, p. 6).

The other side of the approach involves concepts of personal adjustment, namely, the overt behavioral and psychological factors associated with role change. These factors are personal activity and personal life satisfaction. Thus, activity theory makes a distinction between (1) what might happen to *all* aged persons because of the socially-patterned nature of the life cycle, and (2) how persons react both overtly (behavior) and psychologically (attitudes) to later life cycle changes.

What is the structure of the later parts of the life cycle as conceived by this approach to old age? A delineation is made between later life cycle changes in the United States and in other societies (Cavan *et al.*, 1949, p. 10). For example, in some societies the work and/or authority roles held by individuals in middle-adult life continue to be held well into old age. Simmons (1945), in a survey of seventy-one primitive societies, found that stable and sedentary cultures have well-defined and continuous adult roles providing relatively highly functional activities for old people. Although Cavan *et al.* do not mention them, other societies maintain life cycle social integration by providing specific and respected old age roles when adults reach that degree of maturity (cf. Talmon-Garber, 1962). The aged in the United States, however, suffer major role losses without recognized compensations. When persons are "retired," the discontinuity implies more than just the loss of a work role. It involves being in a social situation with no well-delineated status of any kind.

The link between the structure of old age and personal adjustment is located in the self (Cavan, 1962). A person's image of himself develops out of the expressions and judgments of others about him. He learns who he is and the quality of his character through social interaction with others in varied social statuses and roles. At least two levels are involved in the influence of others' judgments on the self. One is a function of the degree of prestige built into the particular status occupied by a person. The other level involves the judgments of a person's performances within varied statuses. Judgments of performances are contingent on holding status.

One implication for self of holding a particular status is that whatever the defined prestige is that is linked to this position, is also the prestige of the self, namely, self-esteem. The influence of status prestige on self-esteem depends on at least two operating factors: (1) a person occupying a particular position must be considered a legitimate occupant, and (2) the occupant must be evaluatively committed to the position.

For a person faced with old age, those social situations and societies having well-delineated age statuses lead to some type of prestige for old persons. Whatever the prestige of old age, it may be translated into comparable self-images (given that the foregoing two factors are operating). Persons in such situations know who they are and are aware of the prestige of their positions in spite of their performances.

Societies possessing no clearly defined roles and statuses for the aged lead to altogether different psychological outcomes.

Here the level of judgments stemming from performances is trivial, since there exist no publicly recognized roles for old people. An aged person in the United States faces such a situation. This means that who he is, what others think of him, and how he is to act remains vague. Such a person is faced with a life situation devoid of relatively structured expectations on behavior.

Given such variations in the definitiveness of roles and statuses for the aged, how do the activity theorists approach the problem of individual responses to situations which emerge from them? The responses of old people are labeled "personal adjustment" (Cavan *et al.*, 1949, p. 11), such responses being directly bound to the control aspects of the self. The argument is founded on Mead's (1934) thinking about self-control.

Self-conceptions have significant implications for the control of a person's behavior. Depending on how he defines himself, the object which is his self will be acted toward as he defines it. If the conception of self that is perceived through significant others is negative, then one's self-regard tends to be negative. Such an individual begins to despise himself and act in self-hate (cf. Rose, 1962a, pp.537-549). If there is little or no socially meaningful definition for old age, the consequent social emptiness leads to a kind of psychological nihilism. Such persons exhibit little directiveness in the control of their behavior. They feel empty and aimless.

Activity theorists conclude that old age in the United States has the following characteristics:

1. Old age roles are not clearly defined.
2. Social situations facing old people in the United States are not well-defined and therefore tend to be anomic.
3. Persons growing old and entering such situations face severe adjustment problems since they leave well-defined roles and enter "undelineated ones."
4. When no well-delineated, socially-meaningful role is substituted for a previously meaningful one, then persons internalize this condition. This leads to alienation and "maladjustment" (cf. Cavan *et al.*, 1949, p. 15).

If aging has such characteristics, its primary issue as a social problem is how to resolve the maladjustment stemming from responses to the absence of meaningful roles. By what means are the aged to be readjusted?

The answer to this lies in the nature of what is defined as a socially meaningful role in America. In the United States, the situation that would be necessary to provide an old person with a "satisfying adjustment experience" (Cavan, 1962, p. 528) would entail two conditions: (1) Acceptance of the value of old age, and (2) creation of publicly-valued roles for the aged. The primary necessity of these roles is that they should be "work-like." The activity theorists are never so explicit as to systematically outline the precise roles which they have in mind, however.

In spite of the fact that they do not explicitly delineate these "adjusted" roles, some semblance of what activity theorists have in mind may be extracted from the discussions of adjusted old persons. Generally, whatever the particular activity, these theorists seem to be urging old persons to continue to be involved in "work" similar to that of their adult working years (cf. Havighurst and Albrecht, 1953; Tobin and Neugarten, 1961). As they would say, one should expand his life and continue to grow as much as possible from middle to old age (cf. Albrecht, 1951; Neugarten, 1965).

Cavan *et al.* (1949, pp. 15-16) provide several examples of persons who are said to have adjusted well to old age. One may adjust his occupational activities to a retirement status, as when a farmer limits himself to gardening. Or an older couple may retire to California or some other state with a concentration of similarly-situated couples. Here one may pursue the "leisure" of avocational hobbies—such things as golf, woodworking, church-related activities, or part-time work of various sorts. Successful adjustment, as the activity theorists portray it, is a life style that is visibly "busy." There is a great deal of concern over what might be called "keeping going."

Presumably, work-like activity in old age functions as a substitute for regular middle-adult roles. Its relationship to self-esteem is the same and operates in a manner similar to the esteem obtained from everyday middle-adult work. Being occupied in work-like activity, the old person is defined as a fully operational individual who, as in earlier life, commands the respect of his status and performance. Such a person's self-conception, being linked to the judgments of significant others, subsequently comes to be defined in terms of the high public evaluation of work and work-like activity.

Although the esteem of work-like activity for the aged is presumably similar to the esteem associated with work in middle-adult life, there is one implicit difference. Activity theorists often infer that the esteem of work-like activity is partially a function of the unique circumstances of the aged, namely, gaining approval for work-like activity performed under dire circumstances. The implication is that an aged individual is performing in a manner similar to a normal adult but is doing so in the face of impending or existing ill-health, financial insolvency, or death of the spouse. Persons who succeed in performing well in this kind of "work" are sometimes referred to as "courageous," "spry," or "having done marvelously for their age." There tends to be a sense of awe in such descriptions made by activity theorists.

> If the widow is to modify her self-image, we must go back again to the conditions under which new self-images arise—the culturally accepted pattern for self-conceptions, and groups of which the widow is a member which will help her achieve a new self-image through their approving evaluation of her change. Fortunately in the case of widowhood, the culture has devised several appropriate self-conceptions. It is important also to recall that the widow usually retains at least some of her old group memberships. She will receive a favorable reflection from her groups if she is courageous, if she attacks practical problems realistically, if she increases her civic or church work, and so forth (Cavan, 1962, pp. 532-533).

One thing appears to be quite evident in the activity approach to aging. It is that the kind of activity defined as socially esteemed is fixed, namely, it is a specific round of behavior with all or most of the following characteristics:

1. It is work-like or instrumental, and not entirely expressive.
2. It is active and visible, i.e. the activity is publicly obvious.

3. The content of the activity is stereotypically middle-class (the successful aged tend to "work at play").
4. Judgments of the successful aged are filled with awe.

There is a Calvinistic aura in the descriptions of success constructed by the activity theorists. They imply that an elderly person may "realize his success of growing old gracefully by his good work." This is activity theory's conception of the "golden years," namely, work-like engagement.

As stated earlier, the concept of personal adjustment in activity theory has two components: the active or overt, and the attitudinal. As utilized by the activity theorists in practice, however, the stated distinction between these components disappears. The focus of their descriptions and analyses of successful aging, as well as their prescriptions for it, dwell almost entirely on overt activity. The attitudinal component is buried in the active one and, in practice, follows from it. Consequently, the implication is that old people who behaviorally adjust to role loss by "actively substituting," "carrying-on as before," or "growing" are content and satisfied individuals.

As in other sociological theories of aging, activity theory has focused on the interrelationship between behavior and a person's self and life attitudes. The principal interpretation of behavior in activity theory has been as *activity*, not usually as social interaction. Concern has centered mainly on the quality and quantity of "work" and work substitutes, not on the quality of social relationships. This is evident both in portraits of the adjusted aged and in behavioral inventories or questionnaires whose contents list items requesting information on activities (cf. Cavan *et al.*, 1949, pp. 149-159; Havighurst and Albrecht, 1953; Maddox, 1963).

Much of the data on aging collected by activity theorists has been obtained from "activity and attitude" inventories. The original Cavan-Havighurst questionnaire (Cavan *et al.*, 1949, pp. 149-159) is divided into two sections. One section requests information on such topics as health, frequency of familial contacts, leisure, and organizational activities. The other taps degree of satisfaction with various aspects of everyday life, from general feelings to specific opinions about relations with one's family, religious interests, and loneliness. Many of the items are quasi-longitudinal, i.e. they ask respondents to compare their degree of involvement in various activities earlier in life (in this case, at age fifty-five) with present involvement.

Overall, the activity approach to aging has continued to be concerned with longitudinal aspects of adjustment in old age. It has stressed the continuation and development of ongoing middle-age behavior patterns into old age, and it has tended to equate what it defines as successful aging with this kind of life cycle development. Most recently, this approach to aging has undertaken actual longitudinal studies in adult social life (cf. Maddox 1962a, 1963, 1965, 1966). Activity theory has always had a strong developmental character, and is at present progressing more determinedly in this direction.

PROBLEMS OF THE ACTIVITY APPROACH

One of the primary theoretical problems of the activity approach to aging hinges on the implicit assumption it makes about the relationship between people's actions and roles. If we define roles to be active patterns of socially expected behavior, then activity theorists assume that persons largely control the types of roles that are available to them as well as the performance of them. Persons, from their viewpoint, are quite free. They assume that it is within any normal person's capacity to construct and develop an adjusted set of active aged roles.

What happens to the theoretical independence of roles and role variations under this assumption? In extreme form, their independence obviously disappears. The distinction between roles and performances in them is eliminated with all social actions becoming performances. And, as is the case in the idea of performance, it is behavior that is executed, controlled, and consummated by an individual with respect to his assessment of a social situation.

Subsuming structured behavior under personal action (performance) is not unique to the activity approach to aging in sociology. It underpins much of the theoretical discussion and empirical work of what has come to be called symbolic interactionism (cf. Blumer, 1969), especially that offshoot of interactionism that focuses on the construction and transformation of social situations (cf. Dreitzel, 1970).

How safe is it to operate under this assumption? It is probably safe as long as the behavior that is being dealt with occurs in relatively unstructured kinds of situations. However, some roles, e.g. economic and authority positions, are likely to be parts of comparatively well-structured situations that are highly stable over time. In these circumstances, individuals are not as free personally to shape performances and develop a life style as activity theorists infer. To some extent this problem that structured social situations pose for action and interaction prompted Gerth and Mills (1953) to attempt a reconciliation between approaches to them.

The limits within which it is safe to make the activity assumption on personal action and roles are narrow enough to pose rather severe explanatory problems for activity theory. These limits are not solely physiological ones. The narrowness for the aged is also a function of poverty and diminishing significant social contacts through deaths.

Prior to retirement the actions and social adjustments of middle-income persons might be amenable to the prescriptions of activity theory. But what of the retired who suffer drastic reductions in income? Such persons are not few in number. They are less likely than middle-income adults to be free to "grow, develop, and personally adjust" to old age. They are more likely to have to resign themselves to the deprivations of aging.

A second problem of the activity approach emerges when it emphasizes developmentalism. Its theorists have generally had an interest in life span activity, particularly from middle to late life. Their approach usually assumes that the understanding of activity and life satisfaction in old age is enhanced by focusing on prior stages of the life cycle. As Maddox (1970) states:

> The relevance of understanding the determinants and consequences of behavior in the middle years of life for understanding the later years of life is being discovered. There is a new interest

in sociological aspects of life cycle events and their interrelationships to challenge the earlier provincial preoccupations of investigators with childhood, or adolescence, or old age (p. 25).

The logic of developmentalism has at least three, and possibly four, dimensions. In most cases, developmental thinking assumes that whatever is developing is doing so continuously, i.e. there is said to be some identity over time in that which is changing. This property enables investigators to *trace* the course of change of some entity and to make statements about it in its various states, which are usually referred to as "stages." Secondly, these continuous stages are conceived as ordered. Considering any three stages as a, b, and c, they may be said to be ordered if they are transitive, e.g. if b occurs after a and c occurs after b, then c occurs after a. When there is a violation of the transitivity principle, it usually is attributed to external events, not to the developmental process itself. Thirdly, the process of growth is usually conceived as one of emergence, i.e. the stages of growth are thought of as having been "preformed," and development is considered an "unfolding" (cf. Etzioni, 1963). The last dimension, the notion of a critical stage, is probably not essential to developmentalism, although it has often been characteristic of it. The critical stage is not identical to an original state containing some program of future events but instead is a period of the growth process that is particularly sensitive to external events. This dimension, then, may not be a necessary aspect of developmentalism per se. In summary, developmentalism has had the following characteristics:

1. Continuous stages.
2. Transitivity of stages.
3. Emergence of a "preformed" program.
4. Occasional reference to stage criticalness.

One major explanatory problem with developmentalism is that it may not easily be taken for granted that events eternal to that which is developing will be stable over time. If, for instance, the life situations of early adulthood and middle age are fairly stable and continue to remain so into the old age of a person, then much of what might be said about old age for that person may be readily forecast from an investigation of his earlier action. As a matter of fact, the business of forecasting in general relies heavily on the steady progress of events. It takes the caveat of *ceteris paribus* very seriously. Now, what if, on the other hand, there is significant evidence that external events change drastically for some persons at a particular chronological age, usually accompanied in short order by other important changes in events. This is certainly the case for the aged in some societies. Activity theorists have outrightly stated that this characterizes the external events surrounding many American persons in their early or middle sixties. Suddenly, these persons find themselves in "retired" circumstances in more ways than one.

What can be made of this from a developmental perspective? There are at least two ways of avoiding the explanatory problem of unsteady external events which, if they were likely to occur and were given serious consideration, would lead to the abandonment of a general theory using developmental logic. One is simply to limit the approach to cases of aging that are not particularly characterized by significant changes in external events at some specific time of the life span. For such persons, the relevance of understanding the middle years, as Maddox (1970) states, for later life may certainly be more than trivial. Of course, if this strategy is taken, the activity theory of development becomes a less general approach to aging than previously. Perhaps one of the reasons that developmentalists usually provide at least technically sound and objective evidence for their propositions is that the empirical situations in which their propositions are verified are stable. When this is the case, no amount of design expertise will ever uncover anomalous evidence.

There is a second way of avoiding the explanatory problems of unsteady external events. This strategy relies on the concept of the critical stage. A critical stage in the life span could be said to develop when external events are changing most drastically. Postulating a critical stage is particularly useful when the relationship between persons and events shows evidence of the following two conditions: (1) persons are highly sensitive to critical events, and (2) critical events consistently coincide with specific periods of the life cycle. The existence of these two conditions tends to fix the empirical reliability of critical stage occurrence.

If critical events do not consistently coincide with specific periods of the life cycle, which would mean that persons are affected by a variety of social situations which differ in the time and intensity of impact on their lives, it appears that postulating critical stages in a developmental approach would unnecessarily multiply the conceptual apparatus needed to understand aging. It is simpler merely to focus on the variety of situations and events that may affect persons. If the effects of and variations in these external events are known, one could predict how a person's life would change if and when he experiences them.

This latter situational approach to the behavior of the aged leads to serious consequences for developmentalism. First, it ignores the idea of self or personal life span continuity, displacing it with a multi-personal conception of human beings. Second, this leads easily to the idea that an individual may not be the same "person" over his life span, making it difficult to forecast behavior from one point in it to another on the basis of information about any single point. And third, it completely refocuses the study of aging from that of persons to that of persons in situations.

In view of the unnecessary complexity of the critical stage strategy, maintaining a strong developmental position in activity theory is likely to lead that approach to aging to a narrowing of its explanatory scope. This would mean that developmental propositions would always assume consistency in social situations. Activity theory, insofar as it emphasizes development, would become a special approach to activity and life satisfaction in old age.

A third problem in the activity approach to the social behavior of the aged occurs in its use of the concept "personal adjustment." The concept underpins circular arguments about the factors making for life satisfaction among old people. The problem of circularity is no doubt partially a result of how personal adjustment is defined. As mentioned above, adjustment involves a restructuring of both attitudes and behavior (Cavan *et al.*, 1949,

p. 11). When an old person is said to be adjusted, he presumably has changed his life style as well as his thinking about being old.

The circularity problem emerges when people exhibit an overt life style that is supposedly typical of adjusted persons. It is said of these individuals that they have successfully adjusted to old age. With this statement, simultaneous inference is made about their mental state, namely, that it is characterized by relatively high morale. However, when evidence of this high morale is provided, it is taken from the round of overt activities that such persons exhibit. Persons not exhibiting the overt activity said to typify working, middle-aged respondents are claimed to be unadjusted (cf. Cumming and Henry, 1961, pp. 16-19).

A fourth problem of the activity approach to aging is the empirical evidence which contradicts its major proposition. At least two documented types of cases of aging do not support the basic proposition of activity theorists that maintenance of a relatively high level of activity leads to adjustment with concomitant high morale. One of the two is a low level of activity coupled with a relatively high level of morale (Gubrium, 1970; Messer, 1967). What makes for this is that some aged persons are located in age-concentrated environments in which the behavior or activity expected of persons is comparatively low. In these environments, old people satisfy normatively-defined behavior patterns with very little overt effort. They need not exhibit "active lives" to be generally satisfied with their living and accepted by local others. Another type of aging pattern that violates the major activity proposition is found among the "isolated aged" (Townsend, 1957, 1968; Tunstall, 1966). These are persons (e.g. the never-married or long-time widowed) who have developed a relatively long-term social isolation as a mode of everyday life. Being fairly isolated or alone is a way of life for these individuals. For comparatively lengthy spans of their lives, they have experienced and exhibited little or no "busy activity." Subsequently, upon retirement, everyday existence tends to remain as usual. If these individuals have been fairly satisfied with their lives previously, there is no reason for this to change in old age.

Another empirical process that is problematic for activity theory develops out of the theory's implication that activity of any kind may be substituted in later life for the everyday behavior of middle-adult life. Weiss (1969) refers to this as the "fund of sociability" hypothesis:

> According to the idea individuals require a certain amount of interaction with others, which they may find in various ways. They may with equal satisfaction have a few intense relationships or have a large number of relationships of lesser intensity. They would experience stress only if the total amount of relating to others was too little or too great (p. 37).

This hypothesis, which is central to activity theory, proposes that a large number of busy, work-like activities filling the lives of the aged can act as a substitute for the usually intense involvement of persons in significant middle-age roles (e.g. spouse, parent, work).

In his study of Parents Without Partners, an organization of spouseless persons who have children, Weiss (1969) explored the "fund of sociability" hypothesis. He found that the loneliness which results from the desolation that occurs at a break in a marriage relationship is not compensated by substituting the "simple sociability" of an organizational membership providing friendships. A person's sociability is not simply quantitative such that he feels satisfied with his life as long as he possesses a certain amount of it. Rather, Weiss' evidence suggests that sociability varies in quality. There are significantly different types of social relationships, which because of their varied qualities and the distinct needs they fulfill for persons, are not interchangeable.

This finding implies, then, that the "gardening, woodwork, and other crafts" which Cavan and associates (1949) portray as leading to adjustment in old age may not take the place of some significant types of activity in which persons engage. The intimacy of having a living spouse is not replaceable by "active involvement." It is more likely that developing a close and personal confidante whom one trusts and encounters frequently is the type of relationship which revives and sustains a former life satisfaction—and this without any overtly active involvements.

DISENGAGEMENT THEORY

Disengagement theory is a functional approach to social interaction and morale in old age which had its beginning in a tentative statement of basic ideas by Cumming, Dean, Newell, and McCaffrey (1960). It emerged as a direct challenge to the activity theory of aging, which Cumming and her collaborators initially referred to as the "implicit" approach to the social behavior of the aged. As they first stated:

> There does, however, seem to be an implied theory of the aging process which underlies many empirical studies. We receive the impression that society withdraws from the older person, leaving him stranded. Many problem-oriented studies are based on the assumption that this tendency can be prevented by various programs for the aged designed to restore a measure of supportive social structures to the individual. We will offer an explicit alternative to the implied theory, namely that the individual cooperates in a process of disengagement which takes place between himself and society (Cumming *et al.*, 1960, p. 23).

In contrast to activity theory, the disengagement approach is built around a single body of concepts. From the activity viewpoint, variations in the social structural aspects of growing old are considered initially as independent of personal responses to structural change. From the disengagement viewpoint, however, both structural and personal aspects of aging are conceived as part of a single, normatively ordered process, namely, disengagement in later life.

How is disengagement theory a functionalist approach to old age? The answer to this question lies in what functionalism has been generally in sociological theory. Functionalist arguments are constructed in such a manner that all behavioral patterns in a system of social interaction are viewed and analyzed in terms of the equilibrium needs of the system of which they are a part. All functionalist statements tend to dissolve individual variations in behavior into a preconceived pattern of systemic adjustment focused around systemic or functional prerequisites (cf. Parsons, 1951).

If we consider two analytically extreme views of persons in social interaction, it is possible to delineate (1) persons as individuals making overtures to other individuals, exchanging acts over time, and (2) persons as actors who are the parts of an ongoing social system which has a structure and operating requirements. These two views are analytically distinct and are alternate approaches to the same empirical instances of persons in social interaction. They do not exhaust the possible views of social interaction (e.g. the symbolic interactionist viewpoint is another), but rather in many ways are extreme opposites among a variety of approaches.

The functionalist view of social interaction considers persons only insofar as they are parts of, and not individuals in, social systems. This means that the explanation of what persons do is derived from the needs and operations of the system in which they act. Moreover, persons' acts are not completely acts in the Meadian sense, i.e. persons are not thought of as considering, weighing, and making their *own* choices about various dimensions of the situations in which they are located. The functionalist view of persons does assume persons to be actor-like (i.e. consider, weigh, and choose behavior alternatives), but the choices that they are assumed to make are normatively defined. Persons, from a functionalist viewpoint, rationally *carry out* socially prescribed behavior.

If it is not persons' acts that maintain social systems, then what does maintain them? Functionalism centers its analysis of system processes on what it calls "functional prerequisites." A system operates so as to fulfill these requirements. If they are fulfilled, then such a system is said to be in equilibrium. Because of the central importance of equilibrium in functionalism, all functional analyses consider the contribution that various social processes make toward maintaining equilibrium. For any given type of behavior, functionalist interest focuses on how such behavior is "functional" for the system in which it occurs. Since certain kinds of behavior are said to be of central importance for system sustenance, other forms of behavior may be judged as "dysfunctional" for a social system.

Explanations of the occurrence of various forms of behavior are related to the concept of system prerequisites. The emergence of various types of behavior is a function of the needs of given social systems in their efforts to maintain equilibrium. Particular social structures and processes, then, are said to function in some manner so as to contribute to ongoing system equilibrium. Analyses of the functioning of various social structures in any social system are a primary functionalist concern.

The major dimensions of functional analysis may be summarized as follows. Insofar as disengagement theory is a functionalist theory of aging, it has the following characteristics:

1. A person's behavior is conceived as normatively defined action.
2. Persons are conceived as *parts* of social systems.
3. The equilibrium of social systems is dependent on the fulfillment of functional requirements.
4. Functional explanation focuses on the "equilibrium fulfillment" or functional contributions of system parts.

Before discussing disengagement theory as a type of functionalism, it should be mentioned that functionalist thinking itself has not been monolithic. There have been variations among functionalists in the emphasis placed upon the foregoing characteristics. Malinowski (1926) has strongly emphasized the functionality of all existing system parts, while Merton (1957) has de-emphasized this by suggesting and exploring the notion of "functional alternatives." As yet, the arguments of disengagement theorists have not been as varied in their emphases.

The first step taken in building the functional theory of aging is making the assumption that disengagement is an essential feature of social life in its later years. Disengagement refers to:

. . . an inevitable mutual withdrawal . . . resulting in decreased interaction between the aging person and others in the social systems he belongs to. The process may be initiated by the individual or by others in the situation. The aging person may withdraw more markedly from some classes of people while remaining close to others. His withdrawal may be accompanied from the outset by an increased preoccupation with himself; certain institutions in society may make this withdrawal easy for him. When the aging process is complete, the equilibrium which existed in middle life between the individual and society has given way to a new equilibrium characterized by a greater distance and an altered type of relationship (Cumming & Henry, 1961, pp. 14-15).

There are, on the face of it, two sides to the disengagement process, the social and the personal. The withdrawal cited above is said to be a *mutual* withdrawal, i.e. it is actively pursued both by persons who are aged and by the others with whom they interact. Aging persons are said to desire withdrawal from social interaction. This is disengagement theory's conception of the "golden years," namely, a graceful personal withdrawal from social life. Likewise, social systems withdraw from the aged. These two sides of disengagement, which are considered *inevitable,* actually are treated as parts of a single, normatively defined withdrawal process. Therefore conceptually, the two sides of disengagement are in fact one. As Cumming (1963) states:

> The disengagement theory postulates that society withdraws from the aging person to the same extent as that person withdraws from society. This is, of course, just another way of saying that the process is normatively governed and in a sense agreed upon by all concerned (p. 384).

As was mentioned previously with respect to functionalism in general, persons are thought of in their capacities as actors, but they are conceived further as acting so as to carry out normatively defined behavior prescriptions (cf. Cumming, 1963, p. 384). They are, therefore, not conceptually independent of social systems.

There is another important aspect to the meaning of disengagement: the process is considered *universal.* Cumming and Henry (1961) imply that what they find empirically and develop conceptually on the basis of American data is equally true of all other societies. This kind of extrapolation is not unique to their arguments, but is characteristic of functional analysis in general (cf. Rose, 1964, p. 49).

The three defining characteristics of disengagement theory may be summarized as follows:

1. Mutuality—persons do not act or construct as much as

they carry out a normatively defined mutual disengagement with others.

2. Inevitability—the system's as opposed to personal needs and interests are dealt with, systemic needs inevitably being fulfilled.

3. Universality—all social systems, if they are to maintain equilibrium, must necessarily operate so as to disengage from the elderly, disengagement being a functional prerequisite to social stability.

The second step in the argument develops the conception of normative disengagement in the context of functional prerequisites. Cumming (1963, pp. 384-385) asks what function disengagement performs for a society. For the United States, at least, the question is answered in terms of the equilibrium needs of society. Insofar as her discussion of equilibrium centers on industrialization, her argument is applicable, she believes, to all modern societies.

Modern societies, in contrast to preindustrial ones, place a great deal of emphasis on "successful" behavior which is based on standards of achievement and efficiency. These behavior standards are part of the body of central and common values of such social orders. Equilibrium is a function of the achievement of high levels of efficient performance by persons in roles emphasizing this standard.

Because the death and morbidity rates of the elderly are excessively high, achievement-oriented positions which are occupied by the elderly allegedly make for performances which are, on the whole, less competent than the performances of younger persons. Consequently, the equilibrium needs which are fulfilled through satisfactory performances in these positions necessitate the disengagement of the elderly from them so as to allow younger persons to take their place. This displacement is said to be functional for the ongoing operation of modern social systems. Therefore, a functional prerequisite of modernity is the disengagement of the aged. This is the major proposition of disengagement theory. Cumming (1963), while not employing the usual functionalist terminology, states this as follows:

In the first place the organization of modern society requires that such competition for powerful roles be based on achievement. Such competition favors the younger because their knowledge is newer. . . . If Americans are to remain engaged in any serious way past the seventh decade, as many observers insist they must, roles must be found for them that younger people *cannot* fill. Only an elaboration of available roles can accomplish this because it is impossible for a society organized around standards of achievement and efficiency to assign its crucial roles to a group whose death rate is excessively high. When a middle-aged, fully-engaged person dies, he leaves many broken ties, and disrupted situations. Disengagement thus frees the old to die without disrupting vital affairs (pp. 384-385).

In some of their more recent comments on disengagement theory, both Cumming and Henry have raised questions about their previous arguments. Cumming (1963) has left some room for possible lifelong engagement by the elderly through her recognition that there are social roles which are "concerned with persistent values" and resist obsolescence because they focus on "timeless values." Such roles (e.g. the clergyman) are said to be primarily socio-emotional and are necessary parts of any society insofar as all societies must manage the tensions that arise within them. Although instrumental roles are central in the functioning of modern societies, socio-emotional ones are still needed. Notwithstanding this slight change, Cumming's argument remains functionalist.

Henry (1965) has been more pointed in his revision of the original disengagement argument. He questions both the inevitability of disengagement and its intrinsic character. Citing cases in the Kansas City Study of Adult Life from which the theory presumably originally emerged, Henry states that for some persons well into old age, the signs of withdrawal do not appear. As for disengagement's being intrinsic, he states that whether or not this is the case depends on how biological the intrinsic nature of disengagement is taken to be. Henry (1965) accepts the emphasis that Havighurst, Neugarten, and Tobin (who are developmentalists) place on continuity in personality development:

. . . personality processes dealt with are presumably not specific to old age, but rather are based in earlier life experiences, and maintain considerable determining power in their interaction with the life events of old age (p. 33).

With this statement, Henry divests himself of the postulates and arguments of the disengagement approach, since that approach subsumes personal variations in behavior under normatively defined ones. He takes a developmental approach to aging, which views social behavior as personally emergent over time, implying that whether or not a person is "disengaged" in old age is a product of lifelong development.

The evidence for disengagement was obtained by Cumming and Henry from the Kansas City Study of Adult Life. The data presented as evidence of disengagement are age-comparisons of various kinds of behavior, ranging from attitudinal "changes" to comparisons of rates of performance of different activities and social interaction among various age groups. A simple decline of some form of activity with age was taken as evidence of disengagement (cf. Cumming and Henry, 1961).

Death is another kind of evidence for disengagement often referred to by disengagement theorists. This is taken as the ultimate form of disengagement and tends to be utilized as a final verification of the theory's major proposition (cf. Cumming & Henry, 1961, pp. 211 & 224-227).

PROBLEMS OF THE DISENGAGEMENT THEORY

As with activity theory, an implicit assumption about human behavior at the center of disengagement theory determines the nature and scope of its explanations of aging. This assumption is not peculiar to disengagement theory but is true generally of functionalism. It is that the relationship between persons and behavior expectations is such that persons act so as to carry out normatively prescribed conduct.

This assumption leads ultimately to a view of human conduct that is completely normatively determined. The social order genuinely appears idyllic and felicitous. Everything seems to operate smoothly and appropriately, persons having no freedom (within the analytic scheme) to perform in deviant manners. If deviance occurs, which for disengagement theory would mean continual engagement well into old age, this cannot be explained within the theory as a violation of its normative assumption. Deviance is not normatively defined. Rather, if deviance occurs, it is said to be a result of individual and not normative processes. And, of course, from the disengagement or functionalist view of aging any individual deviance (or engagement) is not a negative case against its major proposition because that proposition is *not* about individuals per se.

The explanatory problems with the argument, at this point, are twofold: (1) there is a problem in locating deviance in individual (as opposed to social) sources in that deviance or engagement may not be random in a social system, and (2) the disengagement theorists always verify their major proposition. They appear never to be wrong. Let us take each of these separately.

If it is true that there are documented cases of engagement well into old age (Rose, 1964, p. 49; Rose and Peterson, 1965, *passim;* Talmon-Garber, 1962), some of which the authors of disengagement theory themselves cite (Cumming and Henry, 1961, pp. 190-200), then it should also be true that such cases are not linked to particular kinds of *social* positions or *social* prescriptions, i.e. deviance should not be structured (cf. Lockwood, 1967). All of these instances of continued engagement in social positions well into old age should be randomly distributed in a social system since disengagement theory allows no old age engagement to exist as a function of socially defined prescriptions. It can account for deviance (engagement) in a fashion, then. It does so by stating that engagement, if it occurs, is due to something other than what is structured and normative, i.e. it is due to psychological factors—individual choices made in not being ready to choose an inevitable withdrawal—or to individual differences in the activity level from which disengagement begins. These serve to prolong the moment of incipient disengagement (Cumming & Henry, 1961, p. 211).

The problem here is that there is evidence that continued engagement *is* structured and prescribed (Blau, 1956, 1961; Rose, 1964, p. 48; Phillips, 1957; Talmon-Garber, 1962). Maddox (1964) states this in the reverse manner by discussing evidence of the social conditioning of psychological withdrawal. Since this structured type of deviance is empirically prevalent, the universality of the normative proposition on disengagement as stated by Cumming and Henry is called into question. If *both* disengagement and continued engagement are structured, then the entire disengagement argument tends to collapse.

There is a way of saving disengagement theory as a functional approach to aging in spite of the evidence of structured engagement. This is by limiting the scope of the theory. This is the same strategy that was suggested previously for developmentalism in the face of the problem of inconsistent and significant changes in persons' living circumstances in later life. Disengagement theory could simply ignore cases of structured deviance, taking the position that it is an approach to normatively defined disengagement. This, of course, is an expensive victory, for the "theory" would no longer be an explanatory scheme but would become a descriptive framework focusing on the elaboration of varied facets of one type of aging. Its universality now becomes the universality within normative disengagement, making the postulate of universality trivial. This theoretical limitation expands the category of what is not empirically within the scope of explanation. This category now has two classes, namely, individual and structured engagement.

Cumming (1963, pp. 379-381) has reacted to the problem of individual variation in engagement-disengagement by partially relocating the process of disengagement in temperament. She states that whether or not a person disengages depends both upon normative disengagement and temperamental factors. Persons who are temperamentally "impingers" are most likely to remain engaged in later life. While "selectors" withdraw more readily from social interaction. An "impinger" faced with a norm of disengagement ". . . will try to bring others' responses into line with his own sense of the appropriate relationships" (Cumming,

1963, p. 379). A ". . . selector tends to wait for others to affirm his concept of himself" (Cumming, 1963, p. 379). Faced with a norm of disengagement, a "selector" tends to disengage.

Since for both "impingers" and "selectors" the norm of disengagement is operative, this constant factor cannot serve as an explanation of disengagement. Cumming has not succeeded in combining biological and social variables, as she suggests. Rather, this handling of the problem of personal variations in disengagement completely changes Cumming's previous approach to aging. It is no longer a sociological (functional) theory of aging but rather a psychobiological one.

In this new psychobiological approach to aging and dis- engagement, the proposition that temperament is associated with engagement still has to be verified. It cannot simply be stated that they are associated, this serving as an explanation. This would be begging the question of evidence. Moreover, when verification is undertaken, temperament must be measured *in- dependently* of engagement, in contrast to what functionalists are wont to do.

This brings us to the other half of the twofold problem, namely, that disengagement theorists always verify their major proposition. In scientific explanation, it is not enough that verification is empirical. Even if it is empirical, "verification" still may be circular. This occurs when knowledge of that which is said to be doing the explaining is always obtained from that which is to be explained. Scientific verification must not only be grounded in the empirical world, but the conditions under which disproof is said to occur must be stateable (cf. Popper, 1965, pp. 33-39). If such conditions cannot be stated, alleged "explana- tion" becomes tautological and "verification" trivial.

Disengagement as an explanation, in its initial formulation and potentially in its newer psychobiological form, tends to be circular. The *norm* of disengagement is found in the *act* of personal withdrawal. When persons withdraw from social inter- action, the norm is said to be in operation. When persons choose to remain engaged, the norm is said to be inoperative. All forms of engagement are therefore "explained." Here, we have an empirical argument that is tautological. No empirical condition will disprove it. In view of this, then, although the disengagement approach to aging is empirical, it cannot serve as scientific explanation in its present form.

Another problem with disengagement theory is that it explicitly states that the process of psychological and social withdrawal from everyday life is inevitable. Death, being unavoidable, makes disengagement an inevitable process. This is the ultimate basis upon which the disengagement theorists justify the universality of their major proposition. It is trivial, however, to extrapolate an inevitable social disengagement from universal biological death. To say that death is an ultimate disengaged state is to say no more than that death is universal. This provides no clue to those conditions under which social disengagement and death are two different things. However, it is these very conditions that are problematic in a sociological approach to aging. Disengagement theory by itself offers little means by which variations in engagement with different roles in later life can be explained (cf. Maddox, 1964).

Chapter II

A SOCIO-ENVIRONMENTAL APPROACH TO AGING

In Chapter I, we have seen that two rather distinct viewpoints about the social behavior of the aged have come into existence. Although activity theory has not been formulated as explicitly as the disengagement approach, its assumptions about social behavior and their implied propositions have nevertheless served to guide various empirical and practical endeavors focused on aging.

Activity and disengagement theories have been the center of considerable debate in recent years. Some of this debate has focused on assumptions about the process of aging made by each theory. Some has been more concerned with the empirical scope of each with special reference to their relative capacity to account for wide variations in the aging process. This chapter continues the debate. It begins with a discussion of the present state of theory in social gerontology as a function of the emergent competition between various assumptions about the process of growing old.

BEHAVIOR ASSUMPTIONS AND AGING THEORIES

The assumptions of approaches to behavior have the following characteristics:

1. An assumption is a statement about a basic characteristic of the phenomenon being focused upon.

2. The statement is taken as given, i.e. it is not proved.
3. The formulation and verification of arguments demand making such statements.
4. Statements embodying such assumptions are often implicit.

The often non-explicit existence of assumptions has a significant implication for the development of theories. When assumptions remain implicit and/or are not actively questioned, the development of theories tends to remain technical and empirical. Take the two approaches to aging discussed in Chapter I, for instance. As long as the major person-norm or person-role assumption of each remains unquestioned, each approach develops in one or both of two ways. Within each of the two approaches there is a continual process of technical elaboration. When either of the approaches is challenged by a source located in a competing point of view, empirical findings are usually being debated. The two theories of aging do not experience major crises as formulations as long as debate remains at these levels (cf. Kuhn, 1962).

What occurs in theory development when assumptions become explicitly stated and discussed? A largely nonempirical debate emerges which focuses on the structure and limitations of arguments. Suddenly, there begins to be no "official" theory. Debate centers on the comparative analysis of existing theories as competing approaches to a subject. Some data are best handled by one point of view while other data are best explained by another. Moreover, there begins to be a gradual realization that what is known about a particular subject is not the result of a general, cumulative expansion of knowledge about it, but rather is a function of the concurrent accumulation of data from qualitatively differing points of view. It becomes clear that what is known could not have developed logically out of any one of the competing theories alone (cf. Friedrichs, 1970, pp. 150-152).

As for the development of theory in social gerontology, it appears at the present time that the situation is one of competition. There is no dominant paradigm, as Kuhn (1962) would say. Although in the fifties and sixties such dominance might be said to have been represented by activity and disengagement theories, respectively, in those decades there were still a few dissenting voices. For example, as early as 1957, Townsend was dealing with the possibility of relatively inactive (isolated) but high-morale old people. Similarly Rose in 1964 outlined the problems that withdrawal poses for some old people.

Theoretical competition has implications for scientific work. First, as noted in Chapter I, it makes obvious the empirical limitations of an explanation. The realization of such limitations may lead to deliberate reductions in the scope of propositions. For example, research from either the activity or disengagement viewpoint would deal only with parts of the aging process and be recognized as such. Second, both activity and disengagement theories would be recognized as being partial theories of social behavior in old age. Third, the competition resulting from alternate behavior assumptions would necessitate anyone desiring to do research in aging to choose between competing approaches.

As indicated in Chapter I, the assumptions of activity and disengagement theories lead to opposite propositions on the social conditions said to be most conducive to high morale and life satisfaction in old age. It was shown that these propositions can account for certain types of aging processes under special conditions. This was elaborated in our discussion of strategies that might be utilized to retain the two approaches in spite of empirical anomalies. In both cases, retaining the approaches necessitated limiting them so that each became less than general theories of social behavior in old age.

The methodological problem we are left with is that there now exist two partial theories of aging with no conceptual linkage, each useful under certain limited conditions. The question is whether it is possible to conceive a more general framework than either the activity or disengagement approach to aging. If it is possible, these two current theories of aging would become specialized aspects of the more general framework.

If we could answer the preceding question affirmatively, the conceptual linkage between the two partial theories then could be delineated. From the more general framework, we would be able to state the conditions under which either activity or disengagement assumptions would be useful. A more general schema is available to solve this problem, the socio-environmental approach.

SOCIO-ENVIRONMENTAL CONCEPTS

Some of the concepts used in the socio-environmental approach to aging have affinities with concepts in activity and disengagement theories. However, the way in which these concepts are put together in the socio-environmental approach differs from that of the other two approaches. Let us examine the meaning of socio-environmental conceptions and the con-

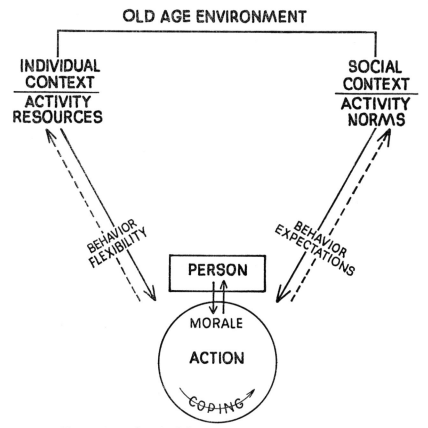

Figure 1.   Schema of the socio-environmental approach.

nections between them. Figure 1 schematizes the major components of the socio-environmental approach along with their linkages.

Old Persons

That aspect of an elderly man's or woman's behavior that takes the individual self and others into account in the process of dealing with his or her environment will be referred to as an elderly *person*. It is characteristic of persons that they *act* toward other human beings as well as toward themselves. To act is first to take account of the significant signals and gestures around a person, be they individual or social. This "taking into account" calls out and influences meaningful dispositions about these signals in a person's mind. A disposition may remain only a tendency or may be actively expressed, according to a person's decisions. The meaningful taking into account of the varied aspects of everyday life (both individual and social aspects), one's dispositions, and the decisions that a person makes are referred to here as *action*. Action is a minded, rational aspect of human behavior. Persons may act with respect to events and others outside of themselves, or they may act toward themselves. *Morale* is a product of a person's disposition toward and judgment of himself. If a person's self-judgments are positive, he is said to have high morale. If these self-judgments are negative, his morale is said to be low.

What implications for measurement does the nature of dispositions have? Do dispositions have certain properties that lead to specific kinds of measurement possibilities? Let us focus primarily on dispositions toward the self as an object. Dispositions, often referred to as attitudes, have at least the following two characteristics: (1) they have both an internal component in the tendency of persons to act in some way toward objects or events and an external component in the expression (active or verbal) of such a tendency, and (2) they may be oriented toward others or toward one's self. The external component of attitudes provides two means by which to measure them: verbal, and active or behavioral.

The measurement of attitudes through verbal expressions (opinions) of self-dispositions assumes the following:

1. It assumes that opinions are indicators of attitudes.
2. It generally assumes relative stability in the dispositions.

An empirical problem of verbal measurement and its assumption of relative attitudinal stability is that shifts in situational influences on self-attitudes tend to be overlooked (cf. Tucker, 1966, pp. 354-357), especially in measurement. The problem here is particularly relevant to the socio-environmental approach to aging, for that approach assumes that self-dispositions are sensitive to the contexts in which they occur, and moreover, builds its theory of action on the basis of such influences on persons. Self-attitudes, from the socio-environmental point of view, are largely an outcome of the contexts that influence them. Thus, attitudes may shift over time from context to context and may not at all be stable. A person may be positively predisposed toward himself in one social context and express such opinions of himself, and be negatively predisposed in another one.

The measurement of old people's self-attitudes through their active expressions (behavior) assumes the following:

1. It assumes that activity is an indicator of attitudes.
2. Specific attitudes are assumed to be influenced by particular kinds of activity.

An empirical problem with these assumptions is that, for old persons, different kinds and degrees of activity may have varied implications for how they will feel, depending on what other persons significant to them expect of their behavior. No particular kind or degree of activity is an indicator of a specific attitude. Activeness may be an indicator of either low or high morale, depending on the activity norms in the context of a person's everyday life. No absolute degree or type of activity can tell us how an aged man or woman will be personally disposed toward himself or others unless the context of his actions is considered. A person's self-judgments are not bound simply to some absolute, active kind of behavior or behavior standard but rather to the social definition and approval of various degrees and/or types of activity by his own particular significant social references.

If one postulates a *simple* and *direct* active-attitudinal relationship, one either may infer a specific attitude for persons with a particular kind of overt activity, or forecast a particular kind of activity from specific opinions. Both activity and disengagement theorists do the former. Activity theorists consider positive self-attitudes to be direct functions of active, overt behavior. The disengagement theorists, on the other hand, state that disengagement leads to a general self-satisfied attitude. The problem with these kinds of inference is that there is a rather long history of evidence (cf. Fishbein, 1967, pp. 477-492) that there is little or no general and direct relationship between activity and attitudes. For one thing, the relationship between attitudes and activity is influenced by the social situations in which they occur. This empirical problem was one of our major criticisms (see Chap. I) of both the activity and disengagement approaches to aging.

From the socio-environmental point of view, persons and their self-dispositions or attitudes shall be taken as situationally and actively variable. The action of persons is contingent on the significant expectations of others within particular contexts of social interaction. Attitudes toward self vary with changes in the contexts of social interaction and emerge out of the individual and social contingencies of these contexts (see Fig. 1). There are two major categories of contingencies in old age, namely, activity resources and activity norms. By assuming that these two have significant effects on self-attitudes, we are setting the grounds for making hypothetical statements on the quality of these attitudes. The socio-environmental point of view assumes some attitudinal stability under constant, contextual conditions. Its approach to persons and their attitudes has some affinities with the interactive approach to Blumer (1969), but it differs in the sense that the socio-environmental approach more strictly isolates significant attitudinal determinants.

In gerontology, two names conventionally have been given to an aged person's global attitudes toward himself and his life style. These are *morale* and *life satisfaction*, respectively. Several scales and indexes have been developed to measure them. One of the first was constructed by Cavan, Burgess, and Havighurst (1949) as part of a study of the relationship between activities and life satisfaction among old people. At least four other, widely used measures have since appeared: the Kutner Morale Scale (Kutner, Fanshel, Togo, and Langner, 1956), Srole's Anomia Scale (1956), the disengagement theorists' morale index (Cumming and Henry, 1961), and the Life Satisfaction Index (Neugarten, Havighurst, and Tobin, 1961). All five measures have been validated to some extent by comparing subject scores with other measures or theoretically related dimensions of behavior. At least two of the measures (Kutner's and Cumming's) checked validity against interviewer ratings of respondents' morale.

Why has morale been a prime area of interest among social researchers studying old persons' behavior? The answer lies to some extent in conceptions of the nature of what action is and how it changes. Action, from its discussion by Weber (1947) through its development by Parsons and Shils (1951), generally has been conceived as a rational, meaningful, and socially-contingent aspect of behavior. This means that the action which is taken by persons is influenced by the social definitions of other significant persons. Since a person's global attitude toward himself, or morale, is an aspect of action, it is influenced by others' definitions of him. Moreover, out of all attitudes, self-attitudes are those which most generally influence the decisions which persons make in everyday situations. Morale or global self-attitudes, then, enter significantly into a person's control of his own behavior.

Because social definitions of behavior change in their impact on persons as they age, such changes have an impact on their morale. Morale, also becomes a salient problem among the aged because their activity resources so often lead to a degree of activeness that is at variance with social expectations. This variance leads to negative self-judgments. In acting toward themselves, persons weigh their abilities as individuals against the expectations of others. The relationship between the individual and social dimensions of a person's environment influences morale. The quality of morale, as a state of self-oriented action, is a result of the balance between the individual and social components of environment in old age.

Environment

The connotation of environment from the socio-environmental point of view is more general than it is in either disengagement or activity theory (see Fig. 1). We have expanded the meaning of environment to include both activity norms (social context) and activity resources (individual context). Disengagement theory conceives of both the person and his environment as parts of a normatively defined social process of mutual withdrawal. Socio-environmentalism does not limit the normative aspect of environment (its social context) to any specific behavior expectations. In activity theory, activity and action are considered synonymous. In contrast to this, we have relegated overt activity (active or potential) to the individual context of an old person's environment. Consequently, an aged person may feel two kinds of factors impinging on himself as a person: factors that are specific to him as an individual, and social factors that constrain him and all others who are like him. Environments may be defined tentatively as follows:

> Environments for the aged are external constraints on persons' actions. The constraints may be social and/or individual restrictions.

This definition postulates several things about the relationship between persons and environments. These include:

1. Environmental contexts are relatively stable in comparison to a person's action.
2. The contexts are objective in the sense that they are conceived as external to and partially independent of the dynamics of mind.
3. Environments are not restricted to the physical space

around the person, e.g. the individual's body is part of his environment.

4. Persons may act so as to alter their environments, either by individual or by collective action.

There is empirical evidence from a study of 210 persons, aged sixty to ninety-four years, who were interviewed in Detroit by the author (hereafter, the Detroit Study) that the aged may feel that their own bodies and activities are parts of the constraints on their lives. An additional reason for conceiving activity resources as an environmental concept is that if a specific group of persons is likely to need to take into account the activity capacities of their bodies in the decisions of everyday life, then it is useful, analytically, to place this "object" (activity) outside of the accounting process itself. It is useful because (1) old persons as a group often cannot easily assume the suppleness of bodily capacity and thus do not so often act "from it" but rather "toward it," and (2) old age behavior norms expressly consider capacity for activity as a restriction on persons.

Two kinds of statements often made by respondents in the Detroit Study exemplify these reasons. Many stated that any time they or their friends decided upon some plan of social activity, they had to take care to remember what they could not do "because this or that person was sick or had some other problem." This was often followed by statements indicating that "everyone here realizes, though, that elderly people have their problems." In short, the aged are more likely than other age-groups to have to consider limitations on their capacity for activity whenever they make decisions about themselves or their social world. Activity in old age is not something that can easily be taken for granted. More likely than not, it is a condition of an aged person's world that is constantly taken into account in his actions.

The socio-environmental approach is a theory specifically constructed to understand the social behavior of the aged. One dimension which makes it a theory relevant to old age is that the individual context is conceived in terms of a factor, namely activity, that is particularly constraining for the aged as a group.. This approach could easily be extended to various categories of handicapped people who have greater limitations than those common to most persons (e.g. the blind, deaf, heart patients, and illiterate). Its usefulness in understanding the behavior of other persons besides the aged depends upon at least two empirical conditions: (1) that persons react to themselves as individuals by feeling constrained in activity (e.g. being physically ill or insolvent), and (2) that they face social situations which prescribe behavior linked significantly to these individual characteristics, i.e. behavior norms assume a certain active capacity to conduct oneself as expected by significant others which a specific kind of person may not have readily available.. If the expectations that persons have for each other's action could always assume a particular capacity for activity, then there would be no reason to delineate activity resources as a condition that constrains people's lives and significantly restricts their decisions as persons. However, because some behavior expectations are not matched by certain capacities for activity among the aged more frequently than among other age-groups, the environment surrounding the old person is conceived as comprised of both a social context (norms) and an individual one (activity resources).

Since there are variations in both behavior norms and degree of activity that may significantly differ in old age, there is a basis for a specifically gerontological theory of behavior. It is not the factor of age itself that is the basis of a theory specific to old age, but rather that certain biological and social conditions are linked to later life in a behaviorally significant fashion.

Activity Resources

Activity resources are one component of an old person's environment. This component places limits on his activity as an individual. For an aged person, three important factors may enhance or limit activity: (1) health, (2) financial solvency, and (3) his state of social support, e.g. having a living spouse. Good health, solvency, and social support are major activity resources.

Old people of good health and/or with financial solvency are not necessarily visibly active or "busy" persons. A person feels and responds to his knowledge of having or not having a potential for activity. Consequently, we are not postulating here that a person's action is influenced significantly only by his overt activity. It is influenced also by his knowledge of what is available to him as activity.

Not distinguishing between manifest and latent resources (i.e. dealing only with manifest resources) is one of the explanatory problems of activity theory. Some activity theorists identify a maladjusted personal state as one of simple inactivity, regardless of whether the inactive person commands the resources to be active. The socio-environmental approach does not ignore this difference.

How is it that activity resources in general affect an old person's action? Depending on their potential, activity resources determine the flexibility to decide upon a course of action that persons have at their disposal. All persons, as they move from one social situation to another, decide upon and demand various kinds of behavior of themselves, to a great extent because various kinds of acts and behavior are expected of them. Whether or not they possess the activity resources to meet these demands will significantly affect their morale and life satisfaction, since the extent of congruency between expectations in any social context and the ability to fulfill them is the condition upon which morale and life satisfaction are based. The personal and meaningful aspect of the relationship between the various demands of contexts is the locus of morale and life satisfaction. If, for instance, the activity norms of a person's social context are internalized by an elderly person, he comes to expect, or to feel he should be able to expect a specific round of activity from himself. At the same time, such a person knows of his individual capacity for activeness, e.g. as one respondent in the Detroit Study indicated, "I know what I can do and what I can't." How a person acts toward and judges himself and his world in response to (1) what is commonly expected of him and (2) his flexibility is that which becomes either high or low morale in relation to himself, or satisfaction or dissatisfaction in relation to his everyday life.

Thus far, several references have been made to both the person and the individual. Let us refer to a person as far as his capacity for activity and the resources that determine its potential magnitude as an *individual*. The boundaries of individuals are roughly equivalent to the activity or potential overt activeness of one's everyday conduct.

Activity Norms

Another component of an old person's environment is activity norms. They emerge in the social context of environments. Because persons are social beings, their acts constructed on the basis of meanings shared with others, they take into account the expectations that are prescribed in their social contexts.

Where do these norms or expectations exist, and how do they operate so as to influence old people? At least three kinds of answers have been given to the first part of this question, one of which is used in the socio-environmental approach.

One way that the question of the locus of activity norms may be answered is by placing them in the *system* of social interaction of which persons are a part. This has been the traditional functionalist answer to the question. It has been extrapolated onto the aged by disengagement theorists.

In approaching the behavior of persons in social interaction, functionalists take the point of view of the system of interaction and its components rather than of the persons acting within them. From their perspective, the central component of social systems is the normatively prescribed behavior expectations. These expectations are part of the system of interaction. Because these norms are located in the system rather than in the person, their relationship to persons has the following characteristics:

1. Norms are taken analytically as given with the system. The question of the origins of expectations is eliminated.
2. They are conceived as operating by normatively defining persons' actions. Persons rationally "carry-out" behavior

prescriptions, becoming equivalent to role performers.
3. Activity norms are located at the core of the system and maintain its integrity.

A second approach to activity norms arises out of analytically taking the point of view of persons as they exchange acts with each other (cf. Homans, 1961). It is probably more accurate to refer to these actors as acting individuals than as persons from this viewpoint, for the system of social interaction existing "between" persons is minimized.

From the exchange perspective, norms are conceived less as constraints imposed on all persons alike than as expressions of valued "returns due" between individuals. In behavior exchanges, individuals come to owe each other reciprocal acts and to expect "payment" for their social investments. For example, if the balance of exchanges has been one-sided between any two individuals for some time, then one of the partners of exchange "owes" the other a debt of returns. Norms are statements about the degree or type of such owing. When payment has been made, what is owed (norms) vanishes. Activity norms, then, can be conceived as overlaying individual person's exchanges, their existence being an outcome of the balance in unconstrained individual actors' exchanges. From this viewpoint, what would normatively occur between old persons and others is seen as an outcome of their owing and crediting each other with certain kinds and degrees of activity (cf. Blau, 1964). Persons come to expect (norm) the activity ("cash") equivalent of their "advances" in exchange (cf. Homan's "norm of distributive justice," 1961).

In social gerontology, the activity theorists come closest to the exchange view of norms. They define the exchanges between persons as normally active exchanges (adjustment). Any two persons, young or old, are bound implicitly by a principle of balanced reciprocity. Because of this, a person is considered as maintaining reciprocal balance in his relationship with others when he returns activeness with activeness. If he is capable of this and acts accordingly, he has completed a social transaction. Activity theorists would say that such a person is "adjusted."

A third approach to activity norms does not deal with the relationship between persons and the social system in the same manner as do the foregoing two. Functionalists analytically subsume persons under behavior norms which are part of social systems. Exchange theorists reduce norms to expectations emergent from the balance of social transactions between individual persons. The socio-environmental approach, however, locates norms both in persons and in social interaction (cf. Cooley, 1964, pp. 35-50). Persons feel "constrained" by activity norms because they commit themselves to and share certain expectations with others about particular behaviors. Their social interaction is guided by shared expectations.

The empirical referent for such norms is that which is expected commonly among persons of themselves. Such norms have at least two characteristics: (1) they exist in persons' minds, the bounds of which are not limited to themselves as individuals, and (2) the shared character of mind implies that these expectations are linked both to persons in relation to themselves and to others with respect to themselves.

In contrast to the functionalist view of norms, the shared view of norms of the socio-environmental approach must attend seriously to how these norms become shared. This is located in the process by which persons in social interaction construct a "working consensus" among themselves. What emerge as norms in some social context, therefore, may be thought of as a form of "negotiated legitimacy" (cf. Strauss *et al.*, 1963). This is what Rose (1965b) had in mind when he outlined some of the dimensions of an emergent subculture of the aged which tends to be generated when old people become behaviorally visible to each other, making for a relatively high probability that they encounter one another and interact. Such a condition exists in age-concentrated social contexts, e.g. in multi-unit housing exclusively occupied by the elderly.

Activity norms, from the socio-environmental point of view, are not systematically fixed. Rather, persons feel bound by whatever consensus about legitimate behavior they have come to accept and share in common with others. For the aged, this means that there is as great a variety of activity norms as there are differences in shared expectations of behavior between persons in various social contexts. From the socio-environmental point of view, there are at least as many potential states of high morale as there are legitimized degrees and kinds of activity which are fulfilled by the elderly.

THE MEANING OF ENVIRONMENTAL CONSTRAINTS

From the old person's point of view, the social and individual contexts of his environment constrain him in different ways. On the one hand, variations in the behavior expectations of social contexts are perhaps best thought of as differences in the burdens placed on persons. On the other hand, variations in the individual context may be considered as a dimension of behavior flexibility from the person's perspective.

The meaning of social contexts may be approached by way of the question of what kinds and degree of burden do various situations place on the aged. Let us take the differences between two kinds of social context, one completely composed of aged persons or age-homogeneous, and the other being age-heterogeneous. In age-heterogeneous environments, the variety of social situations that aged persons are likely to encounter are maximal. There are all sorts and degrees of activity expected by persons of different ages. These range from the comparatively intense activity of healthy, solvent working adults to the relative quiescence of physical invalids. This range of potential activity expectations means that any aged person subject to them must have a sufficient command of himself so as to "make out," as Goffman states, from one social situation to the next. An aged person must be prepared to cope with a variety of expectations, some of which are demanding of activeness while others minimally tax activity. In such age-heterogeneous environments, ability to cope with one situation and its demands does not necessarily mean that one has facility in another. The activity burden in age-heterogeneous social contexts is quite high in the sense that a great number of things may be expected of the aged. Now, what of age-homogeneous social contexts? Here the variety of persons and degrees of activeness that one is likely to encounter are comparatively narrow. The kinds of social situations and expectations with which persons are confronted are few in number. In contrast to age-heterogeneous environments, facility in one social situation in age-homogeneous contexts is likely to mean facility in most.

These variations in the burdens of social contexts are significant in their impact on the morale of persons. Activity resources being equal, morale differences between aged persons are likely to be greater in age-heterogeneous social contexts than in age-homogeneous ones. The life satisfaction of old people here is contingent on a larger number of situations, the average degree of activeness of persons within them most likely being higher than in age-homogeneous contexts. In age-homogeneous contexts, if persons with similar activity resources feel dissatisfied with themselves in one situation, then they are likely to be generally dissatisfied. Conversely, situational satisfaction is likely to mean general satisfaction.

The other component of the environments of old people refers to differences in aged persons' capacities to engage in varied forms of activity. What is the meaning of activity resources for the morale of the aged? Among the aged with extensive activity resources, morale or life satisfaction should be least sensitive to social context variations. In contrast to them, those elderly persons having relatively poor resources, and consequently low degrees of behavior flexibility, should be most sensitive to the conditions of and variations in their social contexts. It is those aged persons who can least afford it that are most likely to be affected by the burdens of different social contexts.

PERSON-ENVIRONMENT RECIPROCITY

Thus, far, in outlining the socio-environmental approach to aging, we have taken old persons' actions as behavior to be explained. Discussion has centered particularly on a person's global evaluation of himself, namely, morale. We have taken the standpoint of the environmental contexts as a perspective on persons' actions. In short, we have discussed the possible independent effects of contexts and their impact on old persons and their morale.

There is another side to the person-environment relationship. This is the facet of the relationship in which persons' actions influence or act back upon their contexts. Analytically, one may choose to probe one side of the relationship and/or the other. What is the nature of this feedback of the person on activity resources and activity norms?

In terms of the analytic scheme outlined throughout this chapter, there are two kinds of reciprocity between persons and contexts. One of these arises out of the relationship between a person's action and his individual activity resources. The other emerges out of the interaction that takes place between persons and others who together hold and share expectations on behavior. Let us examine each of these separately.

Persons and Individual Context Reciprocity

The reciprocity between an old person and his individual activity resources may be thought of as a coming-to-terms with one's capabilities. It is the activity and developmental theorists who have most directly focused on this individual-person relationship in old age. The major point at which the socio-environmental and activity approaches to this relationship differ is that the socio-environmental point of view analyzes the relationship within the constraints of particular social contexts and the activity norms that face an aged person in his everyday life. Let us take an example of this coming-to-terms with one's individual capabilities from the Detroit Study.

An elderly woman whose health had been growing worse since the death of her husband reported that before she had come to reside in her present apartment (located within a multi-unit housing structure exclusively for elderly persons) she felt that her inabilities (her ill-health and the death of her spouse) were going to, as she states, "drive her crazy." At first, she reports, when she related some of her everyday difficulties to her children, they certainly were understanding, comforting, and talked with her about how she might resolve them. But, as it turned out, this sympathetic understanding was short-lived. Her continued references to her inability to "carry on" under the circumstances led to a development of a kind of patronage ("kidding") in her childrens' relations with her. As she states, she began to feel miserable at not being able to ". . . get through to them that I can't keep up anymore and that things bother me that didn't faze me before."

What was happening to this woman was similar to that which Lemert (1962) describes as the initial growth of paranoid behavior among persons. Lemert conceives of this as a process of exclusion that hinges on the magnification of interpersonal difficulties:

> The paranoid process begins with persistent interpersonal diffi-
> culties between the individual and his family, or his work associates
> and superiors, or neighbors, or other persons in the community.
> These frequently or even typically arise out of bona fide or recogniz-
> able issues centering upon some actual or threatened loss of status
> for the individual (p. 7).

Something happens to a person to alter his everyday life—something unexpected, unintended of which he finds himself in the midst. Scheff (1966) refers to this as "residual rule-breaking." The loss of activity resources by our elderly woman leads her to interpersonal difficulties. She has deviated gradually from the expectations of significant others that define adult (and this mother's) capacities as "active" and "self-sufficient." This person is plunged into potentially pathological circumstances. Her dissatisfaction with everyday life grows worse.

One of the characteristics of this process is its non-rational nature. Neither the person who is being isolated nor the persons who are gradually isolating him are initially aware of the general circularity of their actions, albeit all partners to the process consciously contribute to particular aspects of its emergence. All persons become the victims of actions which they have produced in response to each other.

Our elderly woman's everyday life proceeds beyond the

point where she feels the strain of having lost the capacity to perform as an active adult, for she reports that her children no longer "took her seriously." This often leads to a spurious form of social interaction in which persons' minds are not mutually taken into consideration in their exchanges with one another. As Lemert (1962) states:

> Needless to say this kind of spurious interaction is one of the most difficult for an adult in our society to cope with, because it complicates or makes decisions impossible for him and also because it is morally invidious (p. 9).

Now, it should be noted here that although this woman was a "victim of circumstances," she was fully aware of the roots of her difficulties as well as the relational outcomes of them. She was aware of and defined her children's exchanges with her as patronizing. As she reports, "They treat me like a child. . . . No matter how hard I tried, I knew that they wouldn't realize." She slowly began to realize the vicious circularity in the process of growing patronage and exclusion.

The problem for this woman became one of having to cope with interpersonal difficulties when the source of these difficulties (ill-health and spouse death) was unalterable. How does this person react to her individual context? How can she come-to-terms with it in response to the circumstance to which it has led her? In terms of our schema (see Fig. 1), she has available two kinds of choices: either she may (1) begin to define herself as her children see her, or she may (2) alter the social context of her everyday life. If she chooses the first alternative, she is likely to develop an overt and sometimes conscious kind of helplessness. This coping mechanism is not uncommon among the aged, some of whom become skilled at performing as the "children" that they are expected to be. This kind of voluntary dependence accomplishes two things. First, it facilitates inter-action between patronizers and those who are patronized. And second, the dependency of a person upon another may be used by the one to exploit his dependency through acceptance of this subordinate role while at the same time gaining the attentiveness and benefits of others' indulgence. If she chooses the second alternative, her declining capabilities may eventually be accepted as "normal" when it is shared with similarly situated others, provided that she becomes located among and orients herself to such others.

The choice that a person makes, assuming that he tends to avoid sources of life dissatisfaction, depends on the degree of constraint imposed upon him by the social and individual contexts of his environment. In the case of the aged, the constraint of activity resources is often fixed. A person may not be able to alter these. However, there may be a choice that one can make in altering his particular social context, i.e. one may be able to alter the context of his everyday life by moving into an altogether different kind of residential environment. If one does have such a choice, changing contexts may serve to indirectly "alter" the impact of individual resources on self-judgment. If the activity norms of another social context to which one becomes oriented demand relatively little activeness from its occupants, what might have previously been an inactive, low morale individual may become a person whose ability to cope with situations is now adequate. Such a person would grow in morale.

Returning to our example, the woman reported that she had come to know of a local, public residence for elderly persons with "her kinds of problems." She became aware that she might be able to move into the residence. Of course, she did not change her life style immediately. Rather, her coming to reside there was a rather "drawn out and heart-breaking process," as she reported it. In retrospect, she states that she now feels more like "a real person and I am what I am." This as well as other statements made in the interview indicate that her life satisfaction is higher than it was before she came to share her life with other persons in circumstances similar to her own.

Person and Social Context Reciprocity

Let us turn our attention to the interrelationship between persons and others located in one specific social context. In taking action, persons consider the behavior expectations of others in their social contexts. In what way may they, conversely, affect these behavior expectations?

One answer to this question lies in the impact that the spatial relations of persons have on their common expectations of behavior. Rose (1965b) was very much concerned with this issue and has discussed evidence of the growth of a subculture of aging that is an outcome of age-concentration and the emergence of common interests among the elderly as a group. How is the ecology of relationships likely to influence the emergence of certain kinds of social life and their specific expectations of behavior? This problem is an old and difficult one, for it analytically necessitates linking non-minded, "objective" conditions such as proximity and demographic homogeneity to such "subjective" states as group-consciousness, behavior expectations, and morale. An answer to this would indicate one manner in which persons affect the development of behavior expectations or norms.

Considering the chances of encounters between persons, it is likely that they will encounter and interact with each other when at least two ecological conditions exist: (1) when there are other persons available who are similar in social characteristics, and (2) when these others are sufficiently proximate. The same conditions hold for the elderly. The chances of encounters occurring, of course, are influenced also by such factors as the activity resources that persons have available to them as well as the active pursuit by some persons of specific others. However, given persons with similar kinds of activity resources and who are unacquainted, the acquaintance process may be said to be a function of proximity and social similarity.

Suppose that unacquainted aged persons become fairly proximate geographically, i.e. close enough to each other so that the physical energy typically available to a person who may be frail in health and without transportation of any kind except walking may lead to the encounter of another such person on a daily basis. We have in mind, here, residential proximity. On the basis of proximity alone, we should expect that encounters between aged and non-aged persons who are proximate would be similar. The dimension of proximity suggests that the chances of encounters between *any* proximate persons who are unacquainted are greater than among distal persons.

In addition to the dimension of proximity, the degree of

social similarity between persons affects the chances of social interaction taking place. Among unacquainted proximate persons, those who are socially similar are more likely to interact than the socially dissimilar. Proximity has an impact on the encounters between persons, and social similarity tends to transform encounters into interaction. Consequently, there is likely to be age-grading in the interaction that develops between unacquainted, proximate, age-heterogeneous persons.

What is it that leads to an awareness of social similarity on the basis of age? The operation of what Simmel (1955) conceives as the "opposing influences" between groups enhances the awareness of elderly persons that they are a meaningfully and socially distinct collection of persons. An "opposition" influences the awareness of age distinctions in the following manner. Among any persons sufficiently proximate so as to permit social encounters, some are likely to be attracted to each other if a collection of other persons systematically calls attention to them. For the aged, it is probably the case that there would be little awareness among them of the peculiarities of being old rather than young if it were not the case that younger persons make age delineations and respond to them. Proximate aged persons become aware of themselves as a group to the extent that younger persons identify them as aged and make social distinctions along age lines. This identification is a kind of stereotyping process (cf. Berger and Luckmann, 1966). References to the behavior of specific older persons tend to coalesce and become generalized references. Among younger persons who have little or no contact with the elderly, such stereotypes easily reinforce each other in the latter's absence (cf. Shibutani and Kwan, 1965). They have few experiences with the aged that challenge gradually emerging beliefs. This process of stereotyping appears to be unwitting to persons involved in constructing them.

Delineation of the elderly among younger persons becomes increasingly obvious to the aged. Their social interaction and increases in it are direct responses to their growing categorization by an "opposition." This categorization is experienced both in actions and verbally by old people. From their perspective, it is likely to be conceived in conspiratorial terms. There is a vicious circularity to the relationship that develops between the age-groups. This circularity is the inter-group analogue of what Lemert (1962) refers to as "paranoia and the dynamics of exclusion" in the interaction between persons.

The end result of this opposition process is often the development of a particular social context built specifically on the external reactions and internal social interaction of aged persons. The aged, reacting to younger persons, or a growing culture of the young, create and generate age-specific activity norms. A subculture of the aged emerges. If persons in age-specific social contexts or subcultures become conscious of their unique interests in contrast to younger persons, the ground is set for action based on these interests. When this occurs, it might be said in retrospect that one social group has set the basis for and enhanced the growth of another.

As will be shown in Chapters III and VI, there is some evidence that the age-concentration of the elderly is related to the emergence of age-specific subcultures and group-consciousness. The evidence that exists on the general impact of proximity and social homogeneity on the development of social relationships and groups suggests that these same two factors are similarly influencing the aged. The aged are becoming increasingly concentrated into areas of relative proximity and age-homogeneity. As they become more greatly concentrated and are increasingly distinguished as peculiar by out-groups, they tend to construct meaningful social contexts specific to themselves with particular expectations on behavior.

CONCEPTUAL SOURCES OF THE SOCIO-ENVIRONMENTAL APPROACH

Two conceptual sources of the socio-environmental approach are located in activity and disengagement theories. From activity theory, the socio-environmental approach to aging takes the concept of the degree of activeness in an individual's behavior. From disengagement theory, the concept of activity norms is being utilized. Degree of activeness and activity norms are similar kinds of concepts as far as the actions of old people in that they both *constrain* persons' actions in some way.

The socio-environmental approach has three components. It has a normative component. This involves behavior expectations which are shared by persons in social situations. It also has an individual component. Persons differ in the degree of activity of their behavior, i.e. they vary in the amount of overt movement that they can exert as individuals. The third component is personal. Persons consider the meanings that norms and their individual activity have for themselves as well as their relations with others. We are viewing persons' actions as bound by normative and individual contexts.

In activity theory, activeness is the major focus of concern with old people's behavior. The life satisfaction or personal adjustment of old persons is considered to be a function of overt activity. Moreover, persons are conceived as having command over the degree and kind of overt activity that they exhibit over their life spans. As Havighurst (1954) implies, persons are free to cultivate a successful pattern of activities in their middle-adult years which can lead to a high satisfactory transition to old age.

From the socio-environmental point of view, the notion of activeness is understood to be the same as it is in the activity approach as far as overt or visible, individual behavior. In addition to this, it has been transformed in the following ways:

1. Activity is one context of the environment of an old person's actions.
2. Activity is conceptually independent of action rather than being equivalent to it.
3. Activity is conceived as a resource to, or constraint on, persons and their actions. It may be either overt or latent.

It is obvious that the accusation of being "too free" made about the activity approach in the last chapter has been taken into consideration here. Activity now constrains, but at the same time (depending on its magnitude and activity norms) it may serve as a resource for action. From the socio-environmental viewpoint, it is no longer the case that persons cultivate activity, but rather they take their activeness into account in deciding upon their actions.

In disengagement theory, activity norms for the aged were considered to be norms of mutual withdrawal. It was said that in modern industrial societies, the functional requirements of efficiency and competence necessitated the continuity of maximally proficient performances in various instrumental roles. In disengagement theory, a person's actions are defined as coincident with these norms, i.e. a person is not viewed as ultimately free to act in a manner different from that which is normatively defined. Any variation in this is treated as deviant and considered a problem of individual dissension.

From a socio-environmental point of view, norms are understood to have a meaning similar to that which they have in disengagement theory. They are behavior prescriptions shared by persons in social situations. However, the relationship between activity norms and persons, as well as the variability of such norms, has been altered to some degree:

1. Activity norms are not necessarily uniform across an entire society, i.e. there may be variations in norms at various points of the social order.
2. Action is conceptually independent of norms.
3. Norms impinge on rather than determine persons' actions, i.e. persons take them into account in deciding upon their acts, both dispositional and overt aspects.

These three alterations explicitly change the normative determinedness of disengagement concepts. Rather than being "too free," the disengagement approach too strictly limits persons and their actions to that which is socially expected or normative. From the socio-environmental viewpoint, persons do not inherently and inevitably act so as to disengage, but rather they consider the norms of the significant situations in which they are located in the light of what they are capable of doing as individuals—and then act. The ensuing action is thus not only contingent on situation norms and their variations, but also on a person's individual capabilities and his decisions.

The socio-environmental point of view approximates that of activity theory when:

1. Activity norms and social situations are stable.
2. The norms are moderately high activity expectations.
3. A person's individual activity resources allow sufficient flexibility in activity so as to enable him to act as situationally expected.

If these conditions exist in a particular situation, it is useful to make the person-norm assumption of the activity theorists, namely, that persons are free to construct "active and busy" lives in later life and are adjusted when they do so.

The disengagement approach is approximated by socio-environmentalism when the following is the case:

1. Activity norms in a particular social situation prescribe relative inactivity as acceptable behavior in old age.
2. Persons recognize and accept these norms.
3. A person's individual activeness is comparatively low, making him ready to accept norms prescribing relative inactivity.

If these three conditions occur in some situation, subsuming persons and their actions under social norms would be useful in understanding the behavior of old people in it. Knowledge of the norms of disengagement should tell us much of what we would want to know about aging in such a circumstance. Since persons would be expected to disengage, the low activity which they could expect from themselves as individuals would coincide with social expectations. The social approval which follows this withdrawal would lead to personal self-esteem and relatively high morale.

These foregoing two conceptual sources of the socio-environmental approach may be thought of as special cases of the more general framework. As special cases, they remain useful in particular circumstances.

EMPIRICAL SOURCES OF THE SOCIO-ENVIRONMENTAL APPROACH

The socio-environmental approach to old age is a "grounded" approach (cf. Glaser and Strauss, 1967). It has developed upward, as it were, from the exploration of empirical variations in the social behavior of old people. Current approaches to aging have been examined alongside different instances and contexts of growing old. With each examination, the approaches were altered, limited, and various modes of convergence were attempted. In the process of shifting back and forth between empirical instances of aging and alternate approaches to it, what emerged was the socio-environmental point of view. The socio-environmental approach to aging was not "discovered" in the sense of being found in the variety of cases of aging. Rather, it was constructed to conform as closely as possible to this variety of cases. As Glaser and Strauss (1967) state:

> Generating a theory from data means that most hypotheses and concepts not only come from the data, but are systematically worked out in relation to the data during the course of the research. Generating a theory involves a process of research. By contrast, the source of certain ideas, or even "models," can come from sources other than the data. The biographies of scientists are replete with stories of occasional flashes of insight, of seminal ideas, garnered from sources outside the data. But the generation of theory from such insights must then be brought into relation to the data, or there is great danger that theory and empirical world will mismatch (p. 6).

The empirical grounds from which the socio-environmental perspective on aging has been constructed are twofold. First, there has been a steady accumulation of thinking and evidence in the gerontological literature directed at understanding the relationship between social interaction and morale by combining environmental and personal concepts (Blau, 1956, 1961; Bultena and Marshall, 1969; Carp, 1967; Messer, 1967; Rose, 1965b; Rosow, 1967; Townsend, 1957). Second, our analysis of responses from 210 old people in Detroit, as well as observations of their behavior, corroborated the utility of combining both of these types of concepts.

Socio-environmental Studies

Although the major kinds of thinking about old age in the forties, fifties, and sixties were centered on the activity and disengagement approaches to aging, there was some work being done on the effects of differences in environments on behavior expectations, on the one hand, and old person's attitudinal and behavioral reactions to these expectations, on the other. These studies of aged persons attempted to consider more than their behavior as individuals in the face of such common problems of old age as retirement, illness, loss of supportive relationships due to death, relative financial insolvency, and low morale. The studies noted that the reactions of old persons to the problems were not a simple one-to-one relationship between persons and problems. Rather, variations were found in the reactions of persons who had experienced roughly the same kinds of problems upon growing old. Consequently, something other than the problems alone was affecting their responses.

Attempts at resolving the issue of differential responses to common problems and experiences led to the consideration of the *context* of response to these problems. The question of what characterized the immediate social world of persons who were experiencing such events as widowhood and retirement was considered. If it were the case that persons' contexts varied significantly, they might be related to differential responses.

What was the rationale for exploring the context of responses? The concern with context begins with the assumption that persons, as minded individuals, respond to the social meaning of events rather than some "absolute" aspect of these events. Given any two events that to some outside observer would appear to be visibly the same, the responses of persons to both events might easily be different if the social definition of one varied from the definition of the other.

The interpretation of events in everyday life is a highly social process. It is influenced by the persons who stand in a significantly defined relationship with an individual. It is the persons that an individual has "on his mind" in his varied experiences that provide the context of interpretation. Whatever meanings that events have for significant others will be taken into account in the reactions of a single person to the same events.

How does a person take account of the meanings of others located in the context of events? He does this in at least two ways, one of which is taking account in terms of himself and the second in terms of others. If we assume that persons in any social situation are committed to some extent to the attitudes of others in the same situation, he takes their attitudes with respect to particular objects or events into account in responding to such objects or events. This means that the manner in which he interprets events to himself and how he himself subsequently chooses to act upon these interpretations, is influenced by the world of meaning defined by others in the situation of interest. A person takes account with respect to himself by defining himself as a performer of that conduct that is commonly expected in a situation. Consequently, since others in a social situation are regarded as significant, what an elderly person is to himself (i.e. what he believes and judges himself to be, as well as how he chooses to present himself) is a result of what others think he should be and how he should perform.

A person also takes account of the definitions of persons in a situation by considering the actions of those persons themselves. Not only does he respond to himself in terms of the situational meaning of events, but he knows that others are ready to respond to him in a like manner. They expect that he expects, and is ready, to respond to them as such. In any situation in which persons have invested themselves, they are always "double-bound." They are not only bound to themselves via others, but the link to self is reinforced by others assuming that a person *is* bound to himself through common understandings. Occasionally, others do not make this assumption about an individual and thus do not treat him as a person.

This double-edged aspect to the situational meaning of events that are encountered by persons is taken as a significant factor in elderly persons' responses to the problems of growing old. Because of this, environmental studies have taken social context into consideration in analyzing responses. They have approached the context of responses in two ways: (1) by investigating the social implications of the demographic characteristics of persons in such contexts (cf. Blau, 1956, 1961; Rosow, 1967; Bultena and Marshall, 1969), and (2) by directly exploring the unique meanings (subcultures) that events peculiar to old age (e.g. widowhood, retirement) have in certain contexts (cf. Rose, 1965b).

Each of these approaches to contexts considers specific kinds of situational definitions of events in old age. The demographic approach assumes that when individuals have particular demographic characteristics in common, such as age or marital status, and are concentrated geographically, they are likely to interact and share meaning of events common to themselves. The demographic approach utilizes these characteristics as indicators of probable variations in the local social definitions of events. The subcultural approach focuses on the kinds of statements about old age that are made in various social contexts in which the aged reside. This latter approach is primarily interested in whether or not such statements show evidence of different degrees of a consciousness of common interests among the elderly in social contexts with varying concentrations of aged persons.

These preceding studies provide evidence that the meanings of such events as widowhood, retirement, and poverty for old people depends on the social context in which they occur. For, instance, an aged woman may withdraw from or maintain an active social life following the death of her spouse, depending upon how her widowhood is defined in the everyday social context in which she interacts (Blau, 1961). In a context of married persons, she would likely become an isolate, but among other widows she would share a collection of similar experiences. The meaning of widowhood is influenced by the social definitions of others with whom one associates. Responses to widowhood in terms of self-regard are also a product of social definitions.

The Detroit Study

Another empirical source of the socio-environmental approach is data collected in Detroit. A sample of 210 persons, aged sixty to ninety-four, was drawn from three types of social context differing in degree of age-concentration. Extensive interviews were conducted with aged residents in these social contexts. In each of them, observations of various aspects of everyday life were also recorded.

One of the central concerns of this study was the effects of social context variations on persons' reactions to problems of old age. This had its roots in the data of studies mentioned in the foregoing section. Our interest in social contexts led to the elaboration of a social context typology (see Chapter III) and the stratifying of the sample by context. Findings from previous socio-environmental studies were corroborated in the Detroit Study and will be discussed in the following chapters.

It was in the Detroit Study that the utility of expanding the environment of aging to include its "individual context" was decided upon. Not only was the life satisfaction of old people influenced by the persons in their immediate social contexts and the behavior expectations of these persons, but it was influenced also by the activity resources such as good health and solvency which the elderly might possess as individuals. In the Detroit Study, for example, it was found that some old people felt "caught" between the ill-health of their bodies and the intolerance of younger adults. The aged take both the conditions of their individual resources and the conditions of their social world as contingencies of their environments. Life satisfaction or morale, as a state of mind, is significantly influenced by this two-sided environment. The problems of old age are conceived here as the problems that aged persons encounter and "work through" while acting toward themselves as individuals and as social beings.

Chapter III

SOCIAL CONTEXTS AND ACTIVITY NORMS

IN CHAPTER II, reference was made to a variety of social contexts in which the aged are found. A typology of such contexts was constructed as part of the Detroit Study. We will utilize this typology in discussing some of the characteristics of social life among the aged. By so doing, we have a device to locate analytically variations in old age social life. Each of these kinds of contexts has special problems of its own, especially as it is often uniquely situated in urban areas.

Before discussing the characteristics of the social contexts in this typology, let us emphasize one important distinction. We are not taking as synonymous the terms "social context" and "activity norms." Social contexts are a more general conception than activity norms in the sense that they contain certain norms as well as other dimensions of social life. Some of these other dimensions are the structure of social relationships; the homogeneity of the aged population; the proximity of residential units; the protectiveness (or boundary restrictions) of the social context; the setting of social contexts; and the availability of local services such as food stores, laundries, barber shops, churches, and so forth.

Emphasis is being put on the activity norms of particular social contexts because it is these behavior expectations that are crucial in the psychological reactions of persons to themselves. Activity norms are the public pronouncements of what each person should expect of himself. Insofar as each person is a part of this public, such expectations are the standard that he utilizes to judge the merits of his activity. The social psychology of old age, from the socio-environmental point of view, operates with respect to the meaning of norms and activity resources—not with respect to social and individual contexts per se.

The relationship between social contexts and activity norms was discussed to some extent in the last chapter when examining the reciprocity between persons and social contexts. The relationship is such that under certain ecological conditions (i.e. ecological aspects of contexts), activity norms are likely to change and new kinds of norms generated. We have constructed our typology of social contexts on the basis of two factors that have been shown to be conducive to social interaction and the emergence of specific behavior norms, namely, physical proximity and social homogeneity. Let us examine some of the things that are known about the social effects of each of these two factors.

THE SOCIAL EFFECTS OF PROXIMITY

One of the problems of studying the effect of proximity or propinquity on social interaction is that there is evidence that the chances that interaction will occur, as well as of its being maintained over time are also influenced by the similarity (social homogeneity) between potential interactors. Because of this, analyses of the effect of proximity on social interaction necessitate controlling for the effects of social homogeneity in order not to confound their influence on observed interaction. Studies have generally controlled homogeneity by varying proximity within homogeneous populations. The impetus for such studies was, to a great extent, the housing pressures that followed the Second World War. This pressure was coupled with the possibility of planning new housing, a situation having a significant implication for the study of the effects of proximity, along with other housing features, on the lives of residents. Partly because of these pressures, most of the studies of proximity were conducted in the late forties and fifties.

The kinds of social effects being focused upon in these studies were a variety of forms of social interaction. The earlier studies (e.g. Festinger *et al.*, 1950; Caplow and Forman, 1950) were interested in the effect of proximity on encounters and visiting patterns. Later, similar kinds of studies with aged populations were undertaken (e.g. Rosow, 1967) with greater attention being given to friendship.

Festinger *et al.* (1950) studied two student housing projects whose residents were considered homogeneous enough so as virtually to control the effect of this factor on social interaction. Residents shared a fairly similar educational level as well as many of the same kinds of everyday life problems because they were all students. They were also similar in age, marital status (Westgate and Westgate West were prefabricated housing projects for married students), and their incomes were fairly homogeneous. These common demographic factors, of course, influenced the homogeneity of many other facets of the resident students' lives.

The study found that within the student housing projects, the physical arrangement of apartment units had an impact on visiting patterns. For example, from the second floor of the Westgate West buildings there were two stairways to the ground level at each end of a row of apartments. Residents of units close to either stairway were likely to visit frequently—more frequently among near-stairway units than between them. Residents midway between stairways did not as readily exhibit this differential tendency. Festinger concludes that visiting depends on coincidental passive contacts and that passive contacts are influenced by physical and functional distance. Functional distance is measured by the number of passive contacts that the *design* of a building or court encourages, while physical distance is measured simply by distance.

This study shows evidence of the rather strong influence of ecological factors on the behavior of individuals, other things being equal. In both Westgate and Westgate West, a large share of friendships developed among people living in the same court or building. There was an inverse relationship between sociometric choice and the physical distance between units in the same building or court. The same held true on choices outside of a person's court or building.

Caplow and Forman (1950) conducted a similar study of interaction in a homogeneous student housing project operated by the University of Minnesota. In this project, a sample block with fifty units was selected for study which was occupied by married veterans with children. Each family was asked about its relationships with each other family on the block as well as outside of it.

The sample block was composed of twenty-five buildings with two units each, back-to-back. These back-to-back buildings were arranged in five rows, making for four lanes in which the front doors of units faced each other and two end walkways with units not facing any others. Caplow and Forman (1950) describe the social effects of this arrangement:

> . . . the 10 units in each of the 4 interior lanes and the 5 units in each of the end lanes, open onto a common sidewalk. The use of this footway for ordinary traffic, and the obstruction of traffic between lanes by mud, snow, laundry lines, and sundry other obstacles, give each of the lanes considerable identity as social units. The degree of in-lane association is so high that it may almost be taken for granted that any two families in the same lane are acquainted (p. 362).

Whyte's (1956), and later Gans' (1961), study of Park Forest, Illinois also found that the spatial arrangements of living quarters affect social interaction. Whyte states that the size of courts is directly related to the degree of visit exchanges within them. Gans' examination of the same community explored both the influence of homogeneity and propinquity. The combination of these two factors together was more effective in explaining the variation in visits than either alone.

In 1967, Rosow published a study of the effects of housing environments on social interaction among old people. One of the environmental factors in which he was interested was the impact of propinquity on the development of friendships. The sites of his research were apartment buildings in Cleveland selected on the basis of variations in their proportions of residents sixty-two years of age and over. He divided the buildings into high (50 per cent aged at least sixty-two years), medium (33-49 per cent aged), and low (1-15 per cent aged) age-concentrations. Age-concentration was, in effect, also a measure of old age propinquity since the greater the age-concentration, the higher the chances that any elderly person would be a short distance from any other. His findings showed that old people residing in buildings with high concentrations of the aged were more likely than low-concentration residents to visit, associate, and be good friends with their neighbors.

THE SOCIAL EFFECTS OF HOMOGENEITY

Studies of the social effects of homogeneity have had to take into consideration variations in propinquity. Generally, it has been assumed that if persons in any particular locale have fairly similar physical access to each other, the propinquity factor is controlled.

A study by Macris (cited in Gans, 1961, p. 138) of Park Forest, the same community observed by Whyte and Gans, partially addressed itself to the effects of homogeneity on friendship. Macris found that, although tenants and homeowners in Park Forest were physically proximate, there was little visiting between these two particular groups. The differential status and interests of persons in either group were not inducements to building friendships.

Other studies (e.g. Merton & Lazarsfeld, 1954) have shown that background similarities such as income, age, sex, and leisure interests are related to friendship. However, these studies (Merton & Lazarsfeld, 1954; Gans, 1961) have also suggested that values and interests may be more important influences on social interaction than simple background factors, although background factors and values are by no means independent of each other.

There has been comparatively extensive concern with the impact of age-homogeneity on the emergence of social interaction between elderly persons and the development of friendships. Most of these studies have concluded that friendships do indeed tend to be age-graded. For example, Bultena and Wood (1968) found that in an elderly retired male population, friendships took place primarily among persons of the same age. Messer (1967), in a Chicago study of social variations in environmental age-homogeneity, found that the elderly in age-homogeneous housing projects interacted more frequently than elderly persons in public housing with mixed-age compositions. Rosow (1967) found the same in his Cleveland sample.

Other kinds of homogeneity than age similarity enhance social interaction among old people. Blau (1961) found that homogeneous marital status among the aged differentially induces the development of social interaction and friendship. The recently widowed tend to lose friendships that had been sustained previously by a circle of married persons. The degree of friendship-loss sustained by a person upon becoming widowed varies with the number of other similarly situated persons in her proximity. Widows with a substantial proportion of other widowed persons about them tend to develop friendships with each other. Within a concentration of widows, it is married persons whose social interaction is restricted. Rosenberg (1970, pp. 62-71) also found that among the poor (family income less than $3000), the development of local friendships between elderly males was related to increases in the mean age of neighborhood residents. This was not the case among the solvent aged, though.

A TYPOLOGY OF SOCIAL CONTEXTS

As we have seen, there has been a steady accumulation of evidence that proximity and homogeneity affect social interaction. This, of course, does not deny that other social forces such as mutual admiration or mutual consensus between individuals may increase social interaction once it has been initiated. The factors of proximity and homogeneity are conditions that generate "ideal" circumstances for the emergence of interaction.

If these two ecological factors independently influence the growth of social interaction, it should be the case that the degree of social interaction is greatest when they are operating on individuals simultaneously. This, of course, assumes that their combined effect is a positive rather than a negative one, i.e. the interaction between proximity and homogeneity does not tend to cancel the kind of effect that the sum of each of their independent effects would have on social interaction. On the basis of the available empirical evidence on the influence of each factor on social interaction both separately and simultaneously, we may argue that their combination should enhance social interaction beyond each of their independent influences alone.

Before cross-classifying proximity and age-homogeneity, let us dichotomize each of these factors into high and low. We, as yet, have not specified the kinds of operational criteria used in the literature for categorizing each factor. At what distance between residential units and at what proportion of aged individuals in any locale has it been said that cases of either of these two factors are high or low?

The criterion for categorizing age-heterogeneity has varied in existing studies dealing with this problem. Rosow (1967), for example, divided the degree of age-homogeneity of his sample of apartment buildings in Cleveland into three categories based on whether they were less than 15 per cent aged, between one-third and one-half aged, or over one-half aged. Gubrium (1970) used a 75 per cent old age occupancy rate as a cut-off point for high and low age-homogeneity. His rationale for choosing 75 percent was empirical in the sense that it took about that much homogeneity for aged persons to delineate their local environments fairly clearly in terms of age, under similar conditions of proximity.

There have been at least two approaches to the problem of defining categories of proximity between residential units. One approach is subjective. This approach defines proximity in terms of distances which are meaningfully delineated by subjects. Caplow and Forman (1950) used a subjective rationale for categorizing proximity. Their respondents defined living arrangements as communities only under certain limited conditions of proximity:

> It became apparent as the interviewing proceeded that the block itself must be regarded as a community since it was so identified by its residents and possessed a definite internal structure (p. 359).

An alternative approach is to define proximity on the basis of some non-subjective criterion such as "natural" ecological relationships or simple physical distance.

In the Detroit Study, the criterion used to dichotomize proximity into close and distal was whether or not the residential units of aged persons were physically attached so that access to any one of them from any other was possible without having to leave a housing structure. Age-homogeneity was dichotomized on the basis of whether or not adjacent residential units were occupied by less than 75 per cent or by 75 per cent and over with old people. Given these criteria for dichotomizing residential proximity and age-homogeneity, their cross-classification yields the following typology of social contexts:

Type I social contexts have the highest degree of age-concen-

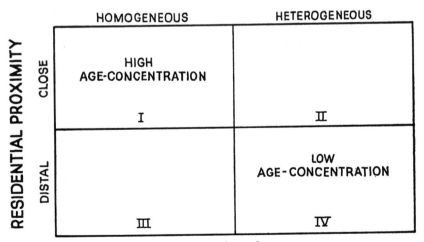

Figure 2. Types of social context.

tration. Here persons live in the same building, residents being comprised entirely of the aged. Among the variety of living arrangements for the elderly, this type has the greatest proximity in its living units along with being age-homogeneous. Type IV social contexts are the least age-concentrated. These are typified by age-heterogeneous neighborhoods of single homes, an extreme form being the age-heterogeneity of a rural or semirural area where proximity is comparatively distal. This extreme may be eventually difficult to locate since such areas are becoming increasingly age-homogeneous, i.e. occupied by the aged. Type II is best represented by multi-unit buildings with a variety of age-groups as occupants and type III by retirement communities such as those commonly found in Florida, California, and Arizona.

This typology, which is built on the cross-classification of two factors has a unidimensional aspect. This unidimensionality is *age-concentration.* Our rationale for this is the evidence discussed above on the influence of the two factors of proximity and homogeneity on social interaction. Social interaction will be said to vary with the age-concentration of social contexts, age-concentration being a function of proximity and age-homogeneity. The evidence that exists implies that the types of social context delineated by our typology may be placed on a continuum of age-concentration from the highest degree of age-concentration to the lowest as follows: I, II or III, and IV. Although Gans (1961) suggests that homogeneity may be a more significant influence on social interaction than proximity, his evidence for this is minimal. Because of this we are not ordering types II and III social contexts in terms of age-concentration.

The foregoing typology is based on two ecological aspects of old age social contexts. The typology is not *ipso facto* a typology of social contexts in general or activity norms in particular. Under the foregoing types of ecological arrangements, variations in meaningful social context are likely to occur. Whether or not socially meaningful contexts do occur is not a simple, direct function of ecological arrangements. As we mentioned earlier, this occurrence is influenced to some extent by the development of an "opposition," i.e. persons outside of the group of elderly who make and act upon age distinctions. Although we will explore this issue of transformation from ecological to social influences on behavior in Chapter VI, for the most part, both in previous studies as well as in our Detroit Study, the transformation has been assumed rather than analyzed.

DESCRIPTION OF THE TYPES

Given that there are four analytic types of age-concentration that lead to the development of different kinds of social context as well as differences in activity norms, what do examples of these contexts look like? The description of these contexts relies on the data of the Detroit Study as well as available evidence in the gerontological literature. Empirically, of course, the character of any description for each type will depend on several factors not part of the analytic scheme of the socio-environmental approach, e.g. the nature of the wider environment such as differences in urban regions, cities, societies, demographic characteristics of the general aged population, etc.

Type I Social Contexts

These contexts, which may be referred to as highly age-concentrated, typically consist of large, multiple unit structures completely housing elderly residents. Their physical boundaries are "natural" in the sense that the contexts are contained within single buildings. The structure itself makes for the close proximity of residents. Moreover, the social effect of proximity is increased or decreased depending on how functionally independent each unit is from any other, e.g. whether there are kitchens within each unit or a common eating area which residents depend upon for their meals. Although there are functional variations between type I contexts, none of these structures is in any sense a nursing or convalescent home since our typology is of the social contexts of the "normal" aged.

In urban areas, it is fairly safe to say that these social contexts are housed in two kinds of multi-unit structures with two kinds of locations. One kind of structure usually did not originally function as an old age residence. These buildings were initially hotels with facilities to satisfy the needs of hotel residents. The other kind of multi-unit structure is built specifically to house the aged. The units in the latter are usually apartments rather than rooms. Apartments are more self-sufficient as living units than are rooms. The location of the hotel structures are usually more central to the major business district of cities since their original purpose was to cater to persons temporarily in that area. The apartment structures, on the other hand, although they also may be centrally located, are more often dispersed throughout various areas of a city. Let us describe cases of each of these kinds of social context from the Detroit Study (all residential names have been coded).

Heart House is a fourteen story hotel-like residence with 200 units located at the edge of Detroit's central business district. Only ambulatory persons over age sixty are eligible for admission. Living arrangements are such that each resident has a private combination living room and bedroom, and a private bath. There is a common dining facility on the main floor and weekly maid service.

Since Heart House is located at the fringe of the central business district, it is a relatively convenient walking distance to varied services. However, in spite of this, the distance also means that persons must walk through the kinds of neighborhoods that are typically near the center of American cities, namely, areas of blight with high crime rates. The immediate neighborhood is populated largely by solitary and transient men and women with extensive unemployment. The area is old and appears quite dilapidated. Although there are other similar residences for the aged located in the same area of the city, three factors make for the isolation of each residence from any other: (1) they are interspersed with slum-like neighborhoods through which aged residents fear walking, (2) the walking distance between some of them is comparatively great, and (3) although most do not have religious restrictions for admission, those that have a religious affiliation are oriented toward it rather than to their common characteristics with other residences for the aged in the area. There is little ecological or social structural impetus for the development of cross-residential interaction.

Another example of a type I context is referred to as West

Side Residences I and II in the Detroit Study. These are public housing facilities for the elderly and are municipally managed. This contrasts with the often private management of the preceding kind of type I context.

West Side Residences I and II are apartment buildings with 82 and 119 units, respectively. They are similar in physical structure, one having six floors and the other nine. Each resident occupies an apartment with living room, kitchen, bath, and separate bedroom. The minimum age for residing in the buildings is sixty years. In contrast to Heart House, some of the residents in West Side I and II were living with a spouse. Persons in Heart House were typically widowed or never married.

West Side I and II are located in single home neighborhoods that have not undergone extensive racial transition. Their vicinities are populated by lower middle and working class families. There is comparatively little crime in the areas. Locally, services are limited to small shopping districts, usually at the intersection of major traffic arteries. Compared to the location of Heart House, the vicinities of West Side I and II do not hinder cross-residential interaction. There is close public transportation available, residents do not as strongly fear walking outside the buildings, and there is public recognition of the ties between the two buildings. This public recognition is a function of at least three factors: (1) both residences are managed in common; (2) although they are approximately three miles apart, residents know of and frequent activities in either building; and (3) personal as well as official references constantly are made to the ties between residents in the two buildings.

Both Heart House and West Side I and II induce intra-residential interaction between persons. In Heart House, residents encounter each other in several kinds of structured situations. The most prevalent of these is eating in common. If not at any other time, persons see each other in the cafeteria three times a day. Other influences on social interaction within this building are (1) a large park-like yard to which there is access only from the building, (2) services such as a beauty shop, small grill, common mail pick-up, small items store, and religious activities room which provide loci for encounters, (3) various all-resident events frequently scheduled, and (4) an all-floor public address system on which residents are informed occasionally of items of local interest.

Although the official structuring of common activity is not as prevalent in West Side I and II as it is in Heart House, social interaction nonetheless emerges from the fact that residents are readily available to one another and age-homogeneous. The extent of social interaction that exists between persons in West Side I and II is more a function of non-institutionally sanctioned influences. Social interaction has its main roots in the characteristics of residents themselves and how they have come to generate an informal round of everyday life. For example, the building lobbies of West Side I and II have developed informally as meeting places. These meeting places have several features: (1) they have territories in the sense that there are specific locations for certain groups, which may be identified by corners, particular seats, or physical relationship to the front door; (2) they are scheduled in that the performances of meetings usually occur at a certain time rather than haphazardly; and (3) meetings tend to be frequented by the same personnel who come to define each other in terms of such events.

Heart House and West Side I and II have formal and informal kinds of social interaction within their buildings. Both kinds of interaction are affected by proximity and age-homogeneity. However, it is the informal kind that is most nearly a result of these two factors alone. In this sense, West Side I and II are the best sites of the Detroit Study in which to consider the impact of close proximity and age-homogeneity on social interaction among the aged. Social interaction in neither kind of type I context, however, is purely a function of proximity and age-homogeneity simply because, in both instances, there has been a deliberate restriction of residence to old people, i.e. these buildings have not become age-homogeneous "naturally."

Type IV Social Contexts

In our typology, the opposite kind of context from that of type I above is one which is age-heterogeneous, the residential-unit proximity of which is comparatively distal. More of the aged live in these contexts than any other type in our typology.

Two kinds of type IV social context have been focused upon in the gerontological literature. One kind may be referred to simply as an age-heterogeneous urban neighborhood of single homes. The other is the mixed-aged rural or semi-rural area. In the Detroit Study, the age-heterogeneous urban neighborhood was dealt with exclusively.

As Marshall (1965) has shown, the continued existence of self-sustaining rural, age-heterogeneous contexts is precarious. In Price County, Wisconsin, for example, the rural farm population aged sixty-five and over increased from 7.9 per cent of the total population in 1940 to 9.4 per cent in 1950 and 10.2 per cent in 1958. The same is true of the rural nonfarm residences in the County, which increased from 8.4 per cent aged in 1940 to 17.7 per cent in 1958. As Marshall (1965) states:

> The meaning of this large proportion of older citizens to the economy of the county is apparent when the income figures for the open-country families (as gathered in the sample survey) are related to the age of household heads. . . . Economically, the cost of services must be borne by a smaller proportion of the population. The high proportion of people in the older age groups also increases the welfare and health problems (pp. 345 and 347).

Marshall found that the oldest residents held the greatest degree of sentiment about the County as well as being least attracted by urban occupations. They were the category of persons that swell the County's population the most. Their educational backgrounds and age simultaneously depress the area. In terms of our typology, rural type IV contexts are tending increasingly to become like type III contexts, i.e. age-homogeneous.

In contrast to the aged in type I contexts whose daily activity involves them with persons other than those in adjacent residential units, the aged in rural areas interact extensively with neighbors. Pihlblad and McNamara (1965) found in their Missouri sample that almost 50 per cent of the aged reported that they visited daily with friends and neighbors in their homes. Physical proximity in rural areas tends to limit everyday interaction to immediate and adjacent units.

What may be said about the effect of age-heterogeneity on

social interaction in rural kinds of type IV contexts? Evidence discussed earlier in this chapter of the impact of homogeneity on interaction would lead us to expect that the degree of local interaction in mixed-age rural areas would be less intense than that in age-homogeneous ones. However, this evidence was in most cases gathered in non-rural areas where residences were close enough so that, at least physically, persons were not limited to contacts with others in immediately adjacent units. The evidence showed that, given the physical possibility (i.e. relatively close proximity), persons tended to interact with others most like themselves. Now, the rural areas, the assumption of unlimited local physical access (at least from day to day) because of proximity cannot be made as easily. Comparatively distal proximity might induce more interaction between neighbors of any kind (e.g. between age-heterogeneous persons) than studies of the social impact of homogeneity in urban areas would lead us to expect. Studies of the combined impact on social interaction of proximity and age-heterogeneity suggest that comparative social isolation exists in age-heterogeneous rural areas. However, because of greatly distal proximity, rural areas, in a sense, leave aged persons with no other choice but to interact with neighbors regardless of age differences, or not interact at all.

As the distance between persons sharply increases, social homogeneity probably becomes decreasingly important in its impact on encounters. When the distance between persons is relatively short, chances are that out of all readily available types of persons, those who are socially similar will interact. When the distance is relatively great, such as in rural areas, there is little or no choice in who is readily available for interaction. Interaction is likely to occur with whomever is closest and not to be as sensitive to social similarity as in urban areas.

An important factor which we have not considered may account for a possible rural-interaction contradiction to the findings of urban studies of the social effects of proximity and homogeneity. This is the impact on social interaction of a high degree of occupational homogeneity. Studies of the influence of age-heterogeneity on interaction do not simply focus on age per se, although age may be the only explicitly operationalized variable of heterogeneity. In these studies, it can be assumed that, because of the retirement pressures of urban occupations, there is probably a major difference between the aged and younger persons besides age that influences interaction, namely, occupational differences and the dissimilar life styles linked to these. Moreover, the differences are compounded by the fact that for persons who ever worked, which includes the retired aged, occupational backgrounds are variable. These urban differences are a rather sharp contrast to the generational structure and variations of rural occupations in which there is not only less of a probability of a definite retirement time that makes age socially crucial, but the occupational backgrounds of rural persons who ever worked (regardless of age) are also likely to be highly homogeneous. This implies that age-heterogeneity in rural areas does not have as strong an implication for other kinds of behavior and demographic differences as in urban areas. The degree of age-heterogeneity in rural areas may have relatively little relationship to differences between persons in what they do, their beliefs, or everyday life problems. Because age-heterogeneity in rural areas may not have as clear a relationship to general social heterogeneity as in urban areas, age-grading of social interaction in rural type IV social contexts probably is not as extensive as in their urban counterparts. The social isolation of the elderly in type IV social contexts is likely to be greater in urban than in rural areas.

The urban counterparts of type IV rural social contexts are, in some locations, as unstable as the latter in terms of the extent of their age-heterogeneity. Although mixed-age urban neighborhoods certainly still exist, it is also the case that many American urban neighborhoods have been and are continuing to undergo population transitions. Transitions are racial, ethnic, economic, and various combinations of these. In the older areas of American cities, it is not unusual to find that the mean age of residents is comparatively high. These areas are occupied by many long-term residents who are also often economically impoverished. To the extent that such urban neighborhoods increase in age-homogeneity, they tend to become similar to type III social contexts.

In the age-heterogeneous neighborhoods examined in the Detroit Study, several features of type IV urban contexts are evident. The daytime differences in activity from one household to another vary significantly with age. Working adults are absent, children are in school, and most of the visible population is either female or retired. Even under these conditions, the aged person is not likely to encounter others with similar interests. As the aged report, e.g. younger women are busily preparing for events later in the day when they are not visiting with each other.

The late afternoon and evening increases the local isolation of the aged in type IV urban contexts. Playing children and adolescents are likely to be avoided, and if neighborhood population is in transition, they are likely to be a source of anxiety. Working adults also have few common ties or interests with the aged. Local relationships between the aged and working adults tend to be limited to the acknowledgment of greetings.

Aside from the fact that the non-proximate residential units of type IV contexts do not structurally induce as much interaction with neighbors as do the multi-unit buildings of type I contexts and that age-heterogeneity also hinders social interaction, another feature of type IV contexts further reduces social interaction. This is racial and ethnic neighborhood transition. This factor, which is more typical of type IV contexts than any other type in our typology, influences social interaction in a manner similar to age-heterogeneity. It is indeed a form of heterogeneity.

As in any type of social context, everyday life for the aged in type IV urban contexts has a routine. This routine, however, is not as institutionally sanctioned as, for example, in Heart House and West Side I and II. Rather, the routines emerge out of the decisions of the aged in these contexts in considering their individual needs and the contingencies of their neighborhoods.

The routines of old age in many urban neighborhoods have become dependent on whether or not there is daylight outdoors. Routines are also comparatively highly sensitive to the weather, since a relatively large share of the elderly walk outdoors to their destinations. The aged have less access to automobiles than the general population (Markovitz, 1971) and are very much limited in mobility to public transit and walking.

The everyday routines of old people in urban neighborhoods are likely to involve them in making walking trips of various sorts such as to purchase small quantities of foodstuffs or other goods at local markets. In her San Antonio sample, Carp (1971) found that 26 per cent of the respondents walked to grocery stores during the day. One-fourth of the sample walked to visit friends. Other walking trips were 23 per cent to religious services, 18 per cent for other than grocery shopping, and 15 per cent to the doctor.

In the Detroit Study, most of the aged reported that they try to be indoors before dark. They expressed concern for their safety when walking to their homes in dimly lit residential areas. Type IV social contexts are not as likely to be immediately adjacent to bus stops or public transportation lines as are the multi-unit buildings of type I. Persons in single home neighborhoods may have to walk several blocks in order to reach public transit pick-up points.

Some of the aged in urban areas have routine "circuits" which they perform on a daily basis. Usually what this involves is the donning of more "publicly presentable" apparel than one usually wears at home. After the daily tasks of the household are completed and a woman has made her public-side presentable, she departs (usually but not always on foot) for her round of visiting points. This may involve a cursory perusal of what may be new in local department or drug stores, a chat with sales personnel who have become acquaintances through sheer daily encounters, and finally a relatively lengthy pause at some point that serves as a rest area as well as a place to have coffee or some other refreshment. This pause tends to be the climax of the "circuit." It may be attended by other daily acquaintances of the same age who converge on the spot from various locations at about the same time.

This kind of routine in non-institutional settings is sanctioned by its participants. Rules of territory and group composition are enforced. Emergent norms may be just as strong in their pressure on persons in these informal settings as rules are in official ones. The difference lies in the fact that participants in informal settings construct and enforce their routines in common.

One major contrast between the boundaries of territories in informal as opposed to formal settings is that of "visibility." In formal settings, the rules for where persons belong are "visible," i.e. they are publicly known or may be known by inquiring about them. This is not as common for informally constructed boundaries and conventions. For the latter, often one must risk breaking these conventions in order to know them. Persons involved in performing informal routines simply are not as conscious of them as they are in formal ones.

Informal conventions exert a rather strong pressure on behavior. Take, for instance, the climax of "circuits" among the aged mentioned above. Old people who are frequenters of the climax will wait for considerable lengths of time if other persons are occupying "their spots." The routine at that point will be temporarily halted until "everyone can take her place." In the Detroit Study, one respondent reported an incident in which she became so exasperated at the length of time she and her friends had to wait that they "just left the place," even though there were other seats available. Routines of this sort become so conventionalized that persons would rather not perform them at all than play them awkwardly. To aged persons who are performers, the "day may be ruined" if routines do not flow smoothly or are not completed.

Type II Social Contexts

Type II contexts are not as pronounced in their impact on the social interaction between old people as are types I and IV. Proximity is like that of type I contexts, but age composition is not homogeneous. This means that although there are persons readily available with whom to interact, these persons are not as likely to have as common interests or everyday life problems as persons in type I social contexts. Encounters between neighbors in type II contexts are likely to occur more often than in type IV contexts, but these encounters are likely to be brief and not develop into friendships.

In Detroit as well as in other studies (cf. Rosow, 1967) this kind of social context was represented by multi-unit buildings usually referred to simply as "apartment buildings." Type II buildings in the Detroit sample were generally smaller than the structures of type I social contexts in terms of having fewer units and floors.

In observing day-to-day relationships in the buildings and in respondents' reports of these relationships, it is clear that social interaction between residents is age-graded. Age-grading also occurs in urban type IV contexts, but in type II contexts, the relatively few aged persons who are locally available are more visible. In type II contexts, tenants that are aged might live across the hall or on the next floor. Encounters are enhanced by such factors as centralized laundry facilities, juxtaposed mail-boxes, or common incinerators. The ecology of these buildings sets high probabilities for encounters.

Elderly persons in Detroit mixed-age buildings (type II social contexts) were well aware of age differences among residents. These age differences entered significantly into their perceptions of and judgments about their surroundings. The elderly readily voiced opinions about building friendships and tenant-manager relationships in terms of age. For example, in the Detroit Study, there were two ways in which the age of residential managers entered the judgments of elderly tenants about their buildings.

Judgments of manager-tenant relationships in these buildings were associated with the age of the manager. In those buildings which had an elderly manager, aged tenants were *generally* positive about their relationship with the manager. Managers were said to be "fine," and "O.K.," or "not a bad old fellow." However, in buildings where the manager was a middle-aged adult or younger, tenant-manager relationships were judged to be strained by elderly tenants. Comments about managers in these latter buildings tended to be more negative in tone.

When the same elderly tenants in these buildings were asked to judge *specific* services within them, the age of managers influenced responses in a different way. Take, for instance, the heat service in these buildings. In most of the buildings, heat is a constant problem for the elderly in the winter months. Since the buildings are generally old, control of the heating system and the flow of heat to all apartments is centrally located. The manager controls heat flow and sets it according to what he feels is satisfactory. When elderly respondents were probed on the specific issue of heat, general comments on managers that were previously expressed, the favorableness of which tended to vary directly with the age of the manager, disappear. On the specific issue of heat, if age enters the respondents' opinions at all, it enters conveniently in defense of their complaints. Respondents in a few of these buildings in Detroit complained bitterly about not receiving enough heat in the winter. "He's freezing us to death," was the usual ending. This kind of complaining was dwelled upon at length by these respondents, almost as if the interviewer could reconcile the heat problem for them, which in some instances he was asked to do. Complaints about the heat occurred regardless of the age of the manager. It was the *heat issue* that was at stake here in elderly tenants' judgments of their residences. In the process of complaining, the manager's age was sometimes referred to. If he were a younger man, he was accused of "doing only for the younger tenants." These respondents then would state that he couldn't know what elderly persons need. If the manager were an elderly man or woman, age references tended also to back-up their complaints, but this time with statements referring to the fact that "he's older and should know better." In this case, a few respondents stated that they just could not understand it.

More often than not, elderly tenants' opinions of younger tenants were somewhat negative, referring to such things as their alleged inconsiderateness, late night hours, or noisiness. A kind of "anticulture of the local young" was constructed by elderly residents. From one respondent to another in the same buildings, similar examples of their complaints about younger tenants were reported. These were shared between these old people and reinforced their beliefs about their common circumstances in relation to younger persons.

Although social interaction between tenants in type II buildings is age-graded, when it takes place it is not as intense or continuous as the interaction between residents in type I social contexts. The chance for interaction developing in type I contexts is greater than in type II in terms of the sheer number of persons with the same interests and problems locally available. For older persons in type I as opposed to type II contexts, the idea of "resident" in general has a different meaning. In type I, "resident" means potential friend or acquaintance. However, in type II, it does not have this potential friend or acquaintance connotation. Rather, "resident" is thought of more in terms of another tenant. What is significant about this is that the connotation of another tenant in type II contexts includes those other tenants in the same building who are aged. Thus, in spite of the proximity and age-homogeneity of some tenants in type II buildings and of all tenants in type I residences, there is a difference in the intensity of local friendships that is influenced by differences in the connotation of "resident."

This difference in connotation which occurs in the minds of the elderly and influences their responses to other old people around them, is not generated solely from variations in the age composition of local residents. Differences in connotation also have a formal source. In Detroit, the type I contexts studied were defined officially as residences for the aged. This means that there was a public influence on the tenant-friend connotation of resident. The type II contexts examined, of course, had no official delineation as housing for the elderly. Consequently, the connotation of "resident" as potential friend in type I social contexts was influenced both by age composition and official definitions, while in type II contexts the latter was absent.

Type III Social Contexts

This type of social context is arranged so that its units are relatively distal. They are not as closely positioned as types II and I in that they are not located in the same building. Proximity is closer to that of type IV contexts. Units are often arranged so that residents have to go outdoors in order to enter other units. They may be patterned in styles similar to urban single home neighborhoods. What makes them different from single home, mixed-age urban neighborhoods is that "neighborhoods" are populated solely by the elderly. Type III social contexts are often referred to as "retirement communities."

Type III contexts were not included in the Detroit Study. These contexts are most likely to be found in warmer climates, especially in the states of Florida, Arizona, and California. They are usually named rather euphorically, having some reference either to the climate or the aged population residing in the communities such as "Sun City," "Youngtown," "Dreamland Villa," or "Green Valley" (Bultena and Marshall, 1969).

Aldridge (1959) studied the social behavior of the aged in one such retirement community in central Florida. Most of the old people in this community were migrants from northern states, which implies that their demographic characteristics are not typical of aged persons in other social contexts. For one thing, the residents of these communities are economically more solvent. Because of this factor alone, comparisons of the aged in these communities with the aged in other social contexts should control for income. Otherwise, any variations in behavior found to occur between contexts may not be a function of the social effects of contexts per se.

In Aldridge's Florida community, a large part of everyday life was structured around leisure activities. However, residents also made a rather obvious distinction between these activities and their own time. Aldridge implies that the maintenace of personal time was of importance to the residents of the community in the sense that there was probably a persistent tendency to over-structure (or overly "activize") their everyday lives. The effort by residents to maintain a distinction between formal and informal activity is one of the most evident concerns of everyday interaction in total or near-total institutions (Goffman, 1961). Retirement communities in some respects (e.g. in their containment of most kinds of services) are more total than type I contexts, residents of the latter sometimes having to leave the confines of their buildings in order to obtain various services.

One particular characteristic of the selection process into

type III contexts is that persons often migrate to them as friends or relatives. Some of the friendships and cliques in these retirement communities, then, are not so much a result of the social pressures of this particular type of context, but rather a function of maintaining prior social relationships. The migration of friends or kin to social contexts is not as evident in type I contexts, which are also age-homogeneous. The ecology of type I contexts more directly affects the development of friendship than does the ecology of retirement communities. Because of these differences, it is probably safe to hypothesize that friendship in type III contexts is more a result of selection factors than it is in type I. In the latter, the environmental effects of proximity and age-homogeneity act upon an initially, relatively friendless collection of persons. This does not mean that retirement communities have no effect at all on friendship patterns. Even though friendships may exist between community members before taking up residence in them, Aldridge (1959) states that these ties are facilitated by the community:

> Cliques also developed as a result of relationships established prior to moving to this community. Many older people came because relatives or friends already lived there, and such relationships tended to become stronger. The newcomer's arrival was facilitated and the established resident's tie with his earlier life was kept alive (p. 71).

The factor of proximity alone is an important difference between types I and III contexts in its impact on the development of friendships. Because retirement communities are so often rather spread out in their layout, each resident in them is less likely to encounter others as readily as in type I social contexts. The lesser proximity of units in type III contexts increases the chances for the development of cliques and sub-communities, which tend to make the total pressure on friendship less than it is in type I contexts. As in other kinds of social contexts similar to retirement communities (e.g. apartment communities housing students), friendships are likely to develop locally such as in the same block or on the same street. The simple distance between residential units, holding age-homogeneity constant, makes it most likely that social ties will be related to proximity.

Retirement communities may develop several internal "neighborhoods." This "neighborhood" breakdown is not likely to be as evident in type I contexts as it is in retirement communities.

The fact that retirement communities are age-homogeneous and are explicitly recognized as a settlement of retired persons is likely to lead most of the elderly within them to recognize the common problems which they face together (e.g. problems of health and social loss). This recognition is characterized by a belief that all old persons may succumb to these problems, that they have an interest in facing them collectively, and that any aid to a person freely offered will be sympathetically reciprocated in times of need. This pattern of mutual sympathy and help also exists in type I social context. It is less evident among the mixed-age residents of types II and IV contexts.

SOCIAL CONTEXTS AND ACTIVITY NORMS

As we mentioned at the beginning of this chapter, the behavior of persons is oriented around and responds to the meanings that social contexts have for them. They do not respond to age-homogeneity and the physical proximity of social contexts per se. In order to trace the impact of social contexts on the action of aged persons, it is necessary to attend first to the mechanisms that translate the behavior influences of age-homogeneity and proximity into something socially meaningful.

Campbell and Alexander (1965) have noted this issue in their delineation of a "two-step" model of structural effects. Because persons are minded individuals and as minded individuals respond to a meaningful environment, any hypothetical relationship between persons and their environments is analyzable only insofar as different environments influence the development of meaningful social situations facing them. Bultena and Marshall (1969), and Rosow (1967) have hypothesized that it is friendship that links social contexts with meaningful situations. Friendship is the mechanism that purportedly translates the social pressures of context into something meaningful.

Proposing friendship as a mechanism has not been altogether a successful hypothesis. If this were in fact the second step in the impact of social contexts on persons, it should be the case that when friendship is controlled in examining the relationship between variations in social contexts and persons' morale (given that persons' health, solvency, and other activity resources are similar), the relationship between context and morale tends to disappear. Bultena and Marshall (1969, p. 8) find, however, that this relationship is only slightly reduced when friendship is controlled.

There is another factor that qualifies as a possible mechanism which translates the physical and demographic aspects of contexts as defined by proximity and age-homogeneity into socially meaningful conditions, namely, the development of activity norms. This has been noted both in Messer's (1967) work on the normative outcomes of variations in environmental age-concentration as well as in the Detroit Study (cf. Gubrium, 1970).

In observing and interviewing old people in various social contexts in Detroit, our initial hypothesis on the link between contexts and persons' socal integration and morale was that friendship was such a link. It was presumed that social contexts varying by age-homogeneity and physical proximity differentially influenced the likelihood of having local friendships. Because persons in particular contexts (age-concentrated) were thought to have more local ties, they were thought to be better integrated into these contexts and to have relatively high morale and life satisfaction. What is it that led us to change this hypothesis?

In investigating this problem, respondents were asked about their friends in connection with the question of how much they felt they "belonged" in their neighborhoods or residences. Answers to this varied widely. Some individuals in age-concentrated contexts (type I) stated that most of their friends were "in the building" or "down the street." Many of these persons felt "at home" in their contexts and "really part of it." They tended to be fairly satisfied with their lives. However, and this is the problem with the friendship hypothesis, other persons in these same contexts but whose stated friends were scattered around the city or country also felt themselves to be part of local life.

Additional problematic evidence emerged when the presumed friendship mechanism was investigated in age-heterogeneous contexts (type IV). Ostensibly, in these social contexts, if the friendship hypothesis was correct, those few aged persons who did have local friendships should exhibit a markedly higher degree of life satisfaction than non-befriended old people. This was found to be the case initially. As a group, the locally befriended aged in mixed-age contexts tended to be somewhat higher in morale than other aged persons. But, their morale did not appear to be of the same *kind* as that of either locally befriended or non-locally befriended high morale aged persons in age-concentrated contexts. The morale of aged persons with local friendships in age-heterogeneous contexts was more the morale of having a "local refuge" in their social environment than a morale of local integration or positive self-regard. These persons were not as much satisfied with their everyday life as they were with having "at least someone else" experiencing similar problems with whom to talk in neighborhoods in which they felt "somewhat out of place."

In exploring the hypothesized effect of different contexts on friendship formation and morale, variations in activity resources were also considered. While examining the morale of the befriended in both high and low age-concentrated social contexts, attempts were made to compare persons with similar kinds of activity resources in order to minimize the possible influence of such factors (e.g. health or solvency) on morale.

On the basis of evidence collected in Detroit, it was concluded that friendship might serve two purposes, depending on type of social context. In type I or high age-concentrated social contexts, friendship serves as a means by which activity norms specific to these contexts are perpetuated. Friendship in type IV contexts (age-heterogeneous urban neighborhoods) provides a means by which aged persons can maintain some semblance of life satisfaction in spite of the fact that they do not express feelings of being part of local everyday life. These two effects of friendship may be referred to as the normative and refuge effects, respectively.

The data were examined next in terms of whether or not a

person's morale was related to local behavior norms. If morale were linked with these norms, a person's references to the state of his general life satisfaction should be coupled with references to local behavior expectations. In type I contexts, regardless of whether a person had few or many friendships, he was more likely than aged persons in other contexts to refer to himself as being "part of" local social life, activity resources being equal. References were typified by the statement that "here people accept you for what you are." As one man stated, "Here, everyone's got some troubles and everyone knows it." For persons in type IV contexts, morale depended on friendship to a greater extent than in type I contexts. For those that were befriended in type IV contexts, friendship tempered life dissatisfaction, especially among persons with poor activity resources.

As we noted at the close of Chapter II, the emergence of norms is a product of at least two kinds of conditions. One of these is group isolation. This is maximized by close proximity and age-homogeneity. Such ecological conditions make it most likely that a group-specific way of living will develop. The other condition is a result of the behavior of persons outside local social contexts. The actions of outside persons which focus on intergroup differences lead to reactions by members of a specific in-group. This makes it increasingly apparent to in-group members that they possess peculiar interests and behavior as a group. Both of these conditions are related to our typology of social contexts. Type I social contexts have a great impact on group isolation, while type IV contexts have less. Type I social contexts are most often characterized as "old age environments" by outsiders, with type III contexts following closely. Type IV social contexts, generally, are known as "regular neighborhoods," with no particular age-distinctions being made.

In each of these social contexts, it is not friendship itself (whether in degree or in kind) that directly influences a person's morale. Rather, it is the shared expectations (norms) among persons about normal and/or appropriate kinds of acts. Friends are important carriers of these norms as well as instrumental in their emergence. However, having friends is not synonymous with knowing of and possessing feelings about particular behavior expectations, once these expectations exist. The knowledge of such expectations and being committed to them may be common to persons without the growth of friendship between them. Friendship is not as much a normative relationship as it is a sharing of particular personal sentiments between individuals. Norms may be perpetuated by friendship, but the impact of norms on persons is not solely contingent on it.

Friendship variations between social contexts differentially influence the development of particular activity norms. Norms, in turn, face all local aged persons whether each specifically has friends or not. Because social contexts differ in the chances of local age-related friendships developing, there are variations between them in the number of active co-operating proponents (friends or primary groups) of particular behavior norms. Once a "way of local life" specific to the aged has developed, however, each resident in a social context considers its meanings and expectations in relation to what he can expect of himself—regardless of the number of local friendships that he has. The significant link between persons and social contexts is not friendship itself, but common behavior expectations or norms.

ACTIVITY NORMS

What are the activity norms in differing social contexts? The evidence for activity norms varying by social context comes from studies of different contexts described in the gerontological literature and from data collected in Detroit. Since types I and IV contexts represent extreme forms of age-concentration in our typology, we will focus primarily on their normative features.

In type I social contexts, elderly persons hold age-linked expectations of each other's behavior. These persons feel that the general non-instrumental activities in which old people engage are a normal aspect of everyday life. Persons are not stigmatized simply because they are not occupied with work. As Messer (1967) states about behavior norms in a public housing project exclusively occupied by the elderly which he studied:

More specifically, older people who are surrounded by "produc-
tive" young and middle-aged people might invidiously compare their
level of activity with their neighbors, perceive that they have too
much free time, and sense feelings of uselessness. Those living with
their age peers, on the other hand, should be more likely to see
leisure itself as an unstigmatized post-retirement activity if age-
concentration is working to produce age-appropriate role expectations, i.e., its own normative system (p. 249).

One kind of statement commonly expressed in age-concentrated social contexts when respondents are asked what a typical
person does in everyday life in them is that he is expected to
maintain some semblance of a cooperative relationship with
others or to simply "be himself." When probed, these people
usually mention such things as taking into consideration the
problems of old age in others, "taking it easy and living old
age," or "making the most" of one's leisure. The norms of everyday life in such social contexts lead to behavior expectations that
are aligned with many of the behavior modifying contingencies
of being old. It is "normal" in these contexts not to work, to be
relatively inactive, to suffer problems of ill-health, to be comparatively insolvent, or to be spouseless.

Consummatory behavior expectations enter into social interaction in type I contexts, and the aged residents of these contexts
are aware that they do. Aged residents not only make statements
about how typical persons act from day to day ("typical" implying normative action), but they also state the implications of
such consummatory expectations for each of their own particular
relationships with other local persons. For example, in Detroit,
it was found that responses to a question about "typical" behavior
were usually followed by comments about sharing common problems of living with neighbors or local friends, or the statement
that "all of us know what you have to face when you're a bit
older."

Not all references to local behavior expectations are negative
in tone. Persons in type I contexts are conscious of the common
local acceptance of "not working." Persons' estimates of each
other are not contingent on their output of some kind of gainful

activity. Rather, individuals do and are expected to engage in more consummatory conduct.

Aldridge (1959), Bultena and Wood (1968), and Hamovitch (1966) all found that similar kinds of behavior norms exist in type III contexts. As in type I contexts, persons in retirement communities accept the consummatory routines in everyday life as a normal run of events. Aldridge (1959) states that this acceptance is linked to some extent with the belief that each person may easily experience problems of old age:

> The older people thought it an integral part of neighborliness to look after each other when necessary. The always present possibility of their own need may have been a factor in this. A woman who had been taking meals for three weeks to her aged neighbor who was ill, said: "I can do that much for the poor soul— she'd do it for me" (pp. 70-71).

The acceptance of consummatory behavior expectations as well as the normalizing of particular behavior problems in types I and III contexts are not a simple matter of "accepting what is commonly believed locally." This kind of "simple acceptance" process would be hard-pressed as an explanation of the relatively extensive influence of local behavior norms on action. Something other than simple acceptance motivates persons in these contexts to consider seriously local behavior expectations in general decision-making and in judging themselves. This other condition is that aged persons in types I and III contexts *invest* themselves in a system of local expectations, and because of this expect returns on their investments. Their acceptance of norms is partially contingent on their trust that if they personally should experience "problems of old age," acceptance by others of such problems will follow as well as others' consideration for the individual difficulties posed by such problems.

The activity norms of type IV social contexts are defined by the typical activity patterns of working adults. This is evident in the expressions of old people residing in these contexts. Many of them feel that they exist at the "fringes" of their neighborhoods, that most other people around them are "busy with their work or their children." Some even state that others "don't have time for the problems of the old folks." A remark not atypical of aged persons in such social contexts is that an old person among younger people feels that he is irritating to them when he "has too much to do with them." As long as associations between the elderly and younger members of type IV contexts are minimal or limited to passing acquaintanceships, the feelings of irritation generally do not enter into interaction. Any more intense kinds of social relationships are usually avoided.

Not only is the normal run of everyday routines in type IV contexts characterized by work activity and local behavior expectations largely defined by such routines, but the elderly often cannot help but to invest themselves in the same system of expectations. Even if it is clear in their minds that they cannot trust such a system to provide them with any returns on its acceptance, the problem is that locally there simply may be "no other market." In such a circumstance, an old person feels that he exists at the whim of local others.

Although the normative system of type II contexts is close to that of type IV, it may not be as stigmatizing for the elderly because the relatively close proximity of residential units makes it less difficult for aged persons to seek each other out. It is easier for elderly persons to find and interact with elderly "confidants" having similar behavior expectations and problems here than in type IV contexts. The social support that comes with having someone readily available in whom to confide tends to ease the impact of local instrumental behavior expectations on old people.

SUMMARY

We began this chapter by outlining some of the existing evidence on the impact of social homogeneity and residential proximity on social interaction. Subsequently, we constructed a typology of old people's social contexts on the basis of the relative influence of these two factors on social interaction. After describing some of the characteristics of four types of context, the question of the process by which the physical and demographic aspects of contexts were translated into personally meaningful entities was raised. Friendship was discussed as being a possible mechanism of translation, but evidence showed that it does not generally influence persons' life satisfaction. Rather, local behavior norms which may be perpetuated by friendship appear more directly to influence life satisfaction. Finally, the activity norms of various types of social context were delineated.

Different activity norms are encountered by persons with various kinds and degrees of activity resources. Not only does an old age environment place demands on persons, but it also provides different kinds of resources with which to fulfill expectations. The resource component of an environment has been labeled its "individual context." In coming to terms with their environments, persons must resolve that which is expected of them with that which they can express. Chapter IV focuses on variations in the individual context of elderly persons' environments. Subsequently, in Chapter V, we shall discuss the interplay of the individual and social contexts of an aged person's environment as it affects his action.

Chapter IV

INDIVIDUAL CONTEXTS AND ACTIVITY RESOURCES

O UR ANALYTIC FRAMEWORK (see Fig. 1) divides the environment of old people into two contexts, namely, the social and the individual. Thus far, discussion has focused primarily on variations in activity norms or behavior expectations from one type of social context to another. In this chapter, the focus shifts to the individual context of old age environments.

THE MEANING OF INDIVIDUAL CONTEXT

Activity Resources

The individual context of a person's environment is that aspect of it which he encounters as an individual, i.e. the capacity he possesses to be actively involved in various aspects of everyday life. The capacity of an individual is a function of many resources. They include satisfactory health, solvency, having the social support of a spouse, relatively high formal education, former occupational prestige and/or occupation-linked social ties, and continued employment. These resources are not mutually exclusive. Continued employment may affect solvency, the expenditures of persons being equal. Or, satisfactory health influences the chances of whether or not one continues to remain employed. Because all of these factors are to some degree dependent on each other, choosing which among them is most significant to the behavior of old people is not a simple matter.

One way to choose between these factors is to move beyond the question of their relatedness and to ask, rather, whether some are more typically problems for old persons as a category than for other age-groups. This is the general manner by which the choice of relevant factors appears to have been made in the gerontological literature. Moreover, the choice of factors on the basis of age-typicality serves to distinguish gerontological studies from other studies of the life cycle.

This criterion of choice, however, is not sufficiently focused to meet the needs of any particular analytic approach to aging. Approaches vary in what each of them defines as behaviorally relevant about old age. Because of this, the socio-environmental approach to aging delineates further on the basis of resources which are relevant to activity norms that apply to the aged.

The criteria of old age and activity norm relevance isolate three factors of significance to the social behavior of old people: health, solvency, and social support (e.g. having a living spouse). Variations in each of these resources influence the activity or potential activity of old people and are relevant to the socio-environmental approach to aging insofar as the norms of social contexts of concern to this approach are activity norms.

That which is significant about health, solvency, and social support for the action of old persons is not the state of each of these three factors alone, but rather the implication of the state of each for behavior flexibility or the possibilities for being active. There is an analytic distinction between the three individual factors, on the one hand, and activity (active or potential), on the other. The three factors together are referred to as "activity resources." Their behavioral significance lies in common implications for flexibility or for an aged person's command over the ability to be active.

This distinction between the factors of old age affecting activity and the behavior flexibility which they commonly influence has not always been made in the gerontological literature. Activity theorists, for example, have tended to treat health, solvency, and activity as relatively independent factors (cf.

Maddox, 1963; Maddox and Eisdorfer, 1962). Respondents in the Detroit Study, however, when asked directly about what conditions influence their happiness, did not conceive of these factors in the same manner:

> Although previous studies of the mental health of old people found that there were strong statistical relationships between health, solvency, activity, and morale, the question still remained whether or not aged persons were aware of and concerned themselves with these factors. . . . The analysis of interview data indicates that health and solvency are perceived by the aged as more fundamental in influencing mental health than activity alone. Other interview data indicate that activity, like life satisfaction, is thought of as an outcome of sound physical health and solvency. (Gubrium, 1971, p. 402).

Most respondents in the Detroit Study emphasized either being healthy or being solvent as crucial to "being happy in life." When asked about whether or not an active person was usually happy, they typically responded by stating that it depended on "how active you have to be." With further probing, most respondents scoffed at inquiries about what they considered the obvious. One man stated:

> Of course! If you got good health, then you can be active or not active—anything you want! Good health is the main thing.

Overall, one may conclude from the data collected in Detroit that activity alone is considered less fundamental to life satisfaction by old people than the potential for activity which is dependent on health, solvency, and social support. To the aged, the ability to be active is a synonym for independence or flexibility, possession of activity resources being basic to whether or not one may be relatively independent in any social context.

Individual Activity Resources

Although activity resources are treated as individual influences on the action of old persons rather than social influences, this does not imply that variations in these resources have strictly individual origins. Certainly, insofar as the problems of poor health, insolvency, and loss of social support are more typical of old people as a group than other age-groups, the origin of these "individual" resources is social.

When we come to the examination of social psychological processes operating among old persons in relation to their life satisfaction, it is useful to treat activity resources as individual entities. The rationale for this is two-fold. First, empirically, within the particular social context he is located, an old person judges what he can expect of himself as an *individual* in relation to that which is expected (normative) in his social context. In the Detroit Study, few cases were found of persons with low activity resources who felt satisfied with their lives in social contexts with high activity norms. Moreover, not one of these few justified his morale by stating that there were other old people alive with the same poor resources in social contexts with high activity norms. Old persons may consider the kinds and degree of activity resources which they share with others, but they typically do so with reference to the activity norms and others within their own social contexts. They do not usually respond to similarities or differences in individual activity resources between themselves and other aged persons regardless of social context. Knowing of the possibility of persons in other social contexts existing with individual circumstances similar to one's own is, save momentarily, not an especially significant influence on a person's action and self-judgment within his own particular social context.

Second, a major concern of the socio-environmental approach to morale is with the person in the face of variations in two kinds of impacts on his life, namely, the influence of activity resources and that of behavior expectations. We are focusing attention on how a person makes comparisons between these two kinds of influence on his everyday life and the personal consequences of their relative congruity. A person's satisfaction with himself depends on the relationship between his abilities as an individual and the behavioral demands of others who are meaningful to him.

RESOURCES AND BEHAVIOR FLEXIBILITY

The relevance for morale of the individual context of an old person's environment is the flexibility that its resources provide him. Because there are variations between social contexts in what is expected of a person, no specific degree of individual activity (potential or active) will always improve a person's morale. Rather, it is the relationship between the flexibility that resources influence, on the one hand, and behavior expectations, on the other, that is important for morale.

The explanatory problem of linking the activity resources of old persons with behavior flexibility is analogous to a similar problem encountered in Chapter III while discussing the relationship between the proximity and homogeneity characteristics of social contexts, on the one hand, and the emergence of particular activity norms, on the other. The problem results from the need to link "objectively" physical aspects of a person's environment (whether social or individual) and subjectively meaningful ones. What underpins this problem is the assumption that there is nothing inherently meaningful to persons in particular kinds of physical and social objects or arrangements. Persons respond to whatever meaning or significance that any physical or social object may exhibit.

The linkage between the physical (proximity-homogeneity) and meaningful (normative) levels of social contexts was handled in two ways. First, the linkage was said to be a probabilistic one in the sense that a consciousness of commonality among the aged was most likely to emerge when they were locally visible and their proximity made the chances fairly high of their encountering each other. Second, the behavior of an "opposition" (i.e. non-aged persons outside local age-concentrated social contexts) is likely to "force" old persons to become aware of their commonalities when it makes invidious overtures toward them. Are there analogous kinds of linking processes between the activity resources in a person's individual context and his behavior flexibility?

Before dealing with this question, a distinction should be made between two facets of the individual context of an aged person, namely, between activity resources and behavior flexibility. The first of these is the objective state of an elderly individual's capacity for activity. Activity resources refer to such factors as health, solvency, and social support. Flexibility refers to the subjectively meaningful state of potential or overt activity which each of the resources influences. From data collected in the Detroit Study, there is reason to believe that, outside of extreme states in any one of the above three factors, health contributes the most to behavior flexibility, solvency is next, and social support the least of the three.

Coping ability refers to the manner in which a person deals with *particular* behavior expectations in his social context within the limits imposed by his degree of flexibility (see Fig. 1, Chap. II). Coping ability is a characteristic of the aged person as he faces himself and tries to deal with others. Confronting the subjectively meaningful aspect of his social context (behavior expectations), a person acts with a certain ability (behavior flexibility) to deal effectively with expectations, i.e. to cope with them.

Data from the Detroit Study suggest that the linkage between resources and behavior flexibility is a result of at least three processes which affect the coping of persons in various social situations. One of these processes occurs in life span changes in coping ability. A person in earlier adult life becomes accustomed to trusting a specific level of behavior flexibility which he utilizes in various ways to cope with problems of everyday life. In later life, there is a probable lowering in the "ceiling" of a trusted amount of flexibility. Insofar as there are changes in the amount of flexibility due to reductions in activity resources, what was formerly simply trusted and thereby largely unconscious becomes vivid and problematic. In relation to that which he could trust himself to do at an earlier stage of his life, he now comes to feel deprived. This felt loss of a taken-for-granted flexibility is an awareness-inducing and meaningful outcome of a reduction in activity resources. Persons become conscious of changes in activity resources as a result of new problems of coping. A taken-for-granted flexibility now becomes subjectively "vivid."

That aspect of activity resources which influences an aged person's awareness of them is not their absolute level of soundness, but rather changes in them relative to an earlier stage of the life cycle. If activity resources had been low throughout the life cycle and remain at the same level in later life, they are not likely to become consciously relevant as a flexibility problem in old age. It is changes in the level of activity resources over the life cycle that results in the meaningful consideration of behavior flexibility by an aged person.

Townsend (1957) found this kind of awareness-inducing mechanism of relative life cycle deprivation resulting from changes in the individual resource of social support. His British data show that persons who are married come to take for granted having a spouse as a source of social support. When such persons became widowed, they felt desolated, lonely, and unable to deal effectively with many everyday problems with which they previously had had the ability to cope. With changes in the individual resource of spouse social support, coping becomes difficult for them. Loss of social support does not occur among those old people who are lifelong single persons. The level of social support which single persons have learned to take for granted and "live with" does not lead to desolation in later life. These persons are not as likely to be as constantly aware of their individual context as far as social support is concerned.

Townsend's data indicate that desolation and problems of coping become personally meaningful in situations involving *experienced* changes in social support. There is evidence from the Detroit Study that an old person who still has a living spouse may *anticipate* a reduction in coping ability, thus making the state of his activity resources subjectively meaningful (behavior flexibility) before any actual changes in them. This is a second process linking resources and behavior flexibility.

How does anticipation operate? It appears that the anticipation of coping ability problems is a function of two kinds of experiences. Some aged persons with a living spouse vicariously experience and become aware of losses in flexibility through the experiences of other persons such as relatives and friends who have lost the support of a spouse. This was made apparent when such persons would pose the questions: "What will become of me if I lose my husband like.......did? How will I manage?" Such anticipation alone leads some of these persons to seriously consider losses of coping ability of their own before they actually have lost through death their own husbands or wives.

Another kind of experience which leads to anticipated losses in coping ability is the chronic or severe illness of a person's own spouse. Such an illness raises the question of one's ability to cope with everyday life without the aid of a spouse. This not only leads to the anticipation of a loss in coping ability, but may lead to greater felt loss before spouse death than after it. One not only may anticipate life without the support of a spouse but must also face coping with (1) his or her own usual everyday problems, (2) those which the spouse had actively dealt with before the onset of illness, and (3) the illness itself. When death occurs, loss of social support as an activity resource operates in a negative fashion increasing coping ability. A living but seriously ill spouse has more negative implications for the behavior flexibility of the person who cares for him than a living spouse per se. Because of the relative gain in coping ability resulting from the loss of a spouse in poor health, the activity resource of having a living spouse must be defined as having the social support of a healthy living spouse. In the Detroit interviews with persons who had lost a spouse in poor health, they typically expressed "relief" when asked about how they reacted to the death. As one person stated: "I hated to see him go, but at the same time I felt like a heavy burden had gone from me."

There is a third social process which links activity resources and behavior flexibility. This occurs in the responses of others to changes in a person's activity resources in the social context of his environment. Given objective changes in activity resources, not only is a person likely to become aware of changes in his abilities relative to an earlier stage of life, but he is further made aware of his activity resources through others' responses to changes in them.

How does this third linking process operate? To a great extent, it operates gradually and unwittingly. When one or more of the activity resources of a particular person becomes impoverished, others do not simply isolate that particular individual from any ongoing interaction between them. The loss of a spouse, for example, does not lead others immediately and decisively to dissociate themselves from the widow. When asked how they felt among their former friends, respondents in Detroit who had become widowed said that they often felt "left out." Further probing into the meaning of being left out did not indicate that others were deliberately acting so as to isolate the respondent. Respondents did not typically consider their former friends and associates as responsible for the growing distance between them. More typically, widowed persons would state that they "just didn't have as many things in common anymore" or that a person felt "like a fifth wheel" among her former friends. Such statements generally were followed by comments implying that it "really wasn't their fault, though" or that "you can't blame them, can you?"

The same kinds of comments were made in exploring the personal impact of declining health. Respondents would say that a person feels that his "health is worse in more ways than one." It was said to affect one's whole life. Various kinds of activities that were in healthier days easily accomplished now are virtually impossible to cope with. As each of these persons in relatively poor health would say about his friends: "You can't expect them to ask you to join in." This was usually followed by: "Of course, it's not that they don't like me—they'd really like me to come along but you know how it is."

Declines in health are defined more negatively than a loss of social support by old persons. Although, initially, both becoming widowed and declining health lead to social isolation, the ensuing isolation may be followed by self-castigation among some persons with declining health. These persons begin to loath their physical state and "hate" their bodies. They consider their bodies as environments in which they are trapped, as if somehow they could rid themselves of it. Their bodies become somewhat depersonalized things.

The growth of a conscious realization of the state of one's flexibility stems from the gradual emergence of social isolation that is not the result of calculated decisions between friends about a person who has experienced losses in activity resources. Rather, the decisions that are made between friends that lead to a person's isolation tend to be situationally induced. Activities planned in certain situations by active participants may not be readily conducive to the participation of persons with limited

capacities. The "forced" participation of low resource individuals
in such situations may lead *initially* to several kinds of temporary
resolutions to interaction awkwardness, e.g. the emergence of
some form of linguistic propriety to "excuse" an individual's
limitations, the behavioral adjustment of timing in activity
sequences so as to allow the inactive to "catch up," and the
development of behavioral "coping aids" to facilitate an individual's performance. The sustenance of any of these resolutions over time involves a great deal of coordinated effort by
group members. It is much easier simply to let the membership
of a formerly active participant "slip by." "Slipping by" is an
important characteristic of the growth of a person's realization of
limited behavior flexibility. The isolating process is a gradual
one. In the Detroit data, respondents at first report feeling
uneasy among friends for some time before they fully realize
the implications of changes in their activity for continued performance in former friendship groups. The dynamics of "slipping
by" are crescive. One respondent described this succinctly as
". . . little things taking place that you don't notice until suddenly
you realize that you're really not part of things."

There are at least two reasons for why the isolation stemming
from a decline in activity resources is gradual. One of these is
that as a group, persons make investments in each other's
performances. This investment means that participants work to
sustain the adequacy of each other's performances since returns
on investments depend upon the soundness of that in which one
has invested. As mentioned above, sustaining adequacy may take
such forms as "making allowances" or establishing "coping aids."
Group members work to sustain another member's adequacy until
they experience diminishing returns on their efforts. Another
reason stems from the more personal components of social interaction. Not only do members sustain their investments as parts
of a group, but they also develop specific commitments to each
other as persons. This personal commitment is characteristic
of friendship. Being a commitment, the personal tie that it sustains is not easily alterable by calculated decisions. Consequently,
any loosening of ties is characterized by gradualness stemming

from the accumulation of situational awkwardness, personal uneasiness, and the difficulty of continual efforts at facilitating the performances of persons having suffered losses in activity resources.

In summary, the links between changes in activity resources such as health, solvency, and social support, on the one hand, and the awareness of behavior flexibility, on the other, are located in three processes. Persons become aware of changes in themselves in comparing their abilities at different stages of their life span. This comparing process makes vivid any behavioral impact of declines in resources. Persons also may become aware of their behavior flexibility through the experience of others. And last, changes in activity resources place a burden upon ongoing social interaction. Because of interpersonal commitments, such burdens may be momentarily tolerated. In the long run, however, an inadvertent process of social isolation typically emerges. The realization of declines in activity resources stemming from social isolation reinforces a person's life span comparisons of his abilities. It increases the transformation of the state of activity resources into the awareness of personal behavior flexibility.

PRECARIOUS FLEXIBILITY AND FEAR

Fear is a state of mind characterized by feelings of anxiousness and desperation (cf. Milner, 1949; Pederson, 1946). Such feelings stem from two kinds of social situational conditions, namely, the unpredictability of events and personal ineffectiveness in influencing the outcome of events when they occur. The activity resources focused upon here have the characteristic that, in old age, they are relatively highly susceptible to change and such change is often unpredictable and unalterable.

Given that the activity resources of health, solvency, and social support in old age are highly susceptible to change, largely unpredictable, and relatively unalterable, it should not be surprising that when asked whether or not they have any fears, the aged respond that they do and that it is related to the precarious state of activity resources and behavior flexibility in their lives.

Such responses were typical of elderly people interviewed in Detroit.

What is the place of fear and how does it operate in the transformation of changes in activity resources into the awareness of changes in flexibility? Since fear is a meaningful state of mind, it exists in persons and not in their individual contexts. This is not to deny, however, that elderly persons define some of the sources of their fears as located in such contexts. How do individual sources of fear become personally meaningful and spawn fear as a state of mind?

Fear arises as a personal state of mind after the emergence of awareness of problems of coping ability in particular social contexts. The sequence of events between changes in an individual context and the emergence of fear is that (1) changes in activity resources occur making for (2) problems in coping with the contingencies of social interaction in various situations, which then leads to (3) awareness of the precariousness of one's behavior flexibility and (4) fear. Fear is a personal response to awareness of problems in coping ability, whether or not this awareness is vicarious or the result of actual experiences. Because it emerges as a response to problems in the ability to cope with issues of everyday life, fear is related to changes in activity resources.

How do old persons actively respond to the fear that emerges with losses in coping ability (real or vicarious)? Data from the Detroit Study indicate that the aged respond by taking what they often refer to as "precautions." This is typically an active pattern of self-control that results in curbs being placed on certain kinds of personal activity. The process of taking precautions operates in the following manner. When persons become fearful of the state of their coping ability (whether personally experienced or vicarious), they tend to inhibit the reoccurrence of whatever relevant activity in which they were engaged at the time and place that fear developed. For example, if the source of fear is located in precarious health and a person was involved in washing windows at or close to the time of fear arousal, then window washing as an activity is likely to be curbed. This kind of activity inhibition occurs even in those instances in which persons become vicariously fearful through the experience of others.

Even though the future state of coping ability may be unpredictable, this does not mean that persons do not act in some manner so as to gain *practical* assurance of being reasonably safe from further declines in resources. Success at gaining practical assurance of safety is a resolution to the intolerable pressure that not knowing the course of everyday events places on persons. It becomes a next-to-best solution to anxiety, namely, it provides some indication that at least one is not contributing to the enhancement of possibly, but not necessarily declining resources. As two respondents mentioned: "Of course you don't know! But why should I make it any worse for myself." And, "At least if I don't climb ladders, then there's that much less chance of a stroke, don't you see."

HEALTH AND FLEXIBILITY

Thus far in the discussion of the individual context of old age environments, varied aspects of the processes of personal interaction with activity resources and flexibility have been delineated. We focused on some of the mechanisms linking resources with the awareness of behavior flexibility and noted how elderly persons respond to active or potential declines in behavior flexibility. Given that the state of activity resources may meaningfully influence old people, what is known statistically about the relationship between activity resources and behavior flexibility? For most statistical studies in the gerontological literature, this has been a question of the relationship between particular kinds of resources and levels of activity.

Two measures of health have been used in studies of the relationship between health and activity. One of these is objective in that indexes of health are based on the responses of subjects to lists of possible health problems. This sort of measure does not focus on how a person perceives his overall state of health but rather is based on a person's recognition of a collection of symptoms and/or diseases presented to him of which he might or might not be actively aware (cf. Cavan *et al.*, 1949, p. 150). Another variation of the objective measure of health is based on the professional evaluation of a person's health (cf. Maddox and Eisdorfer, 1962). A physician or other medical practitioner classifies subjects into various categories of health status. Objective measures of health also have been compiled from frequency of contact with medical personnel or facilities (Scotch and Richardson, 1966), time spent in convalescence (Beyer and Wahl, 1964), and degree of behavior incapacity (Shanas *et al.*, 1968, pp. 26-30).

The other technique of measuring health status is best described as subjective. Rather than typically being indexes of compiled responses to some listing of symptoms, medical contacts, and so forth, subjective measures involve asking respondents a direct question on the state of their health, e.g. asking them how they would rate their health at any particular time. This is usually a closed-end question which is followed by several alternative response categories that range from very poor to excellent (cf. Cavan *et al.*, 1949, p. 150; Maddox, 1963; Shanas, 1962).

Whether or not an objective or subjective measure of health is utilized depends upon the nature and requirements of the study being performed (Shanas *et al.*, 1968, p. 25). Other than on the basis of this criterion, it would be difficult to judge the comparative value of either approach to measuring health as an activity resource. If the study of old people is primarily concerned with their personal behavior and/or personal states of mind (e.g. life satisfaction or morale) as it relates to their health in terms of how persons deal with problems of health, then it would be useful to select a type of health measure that focuses on the personal meaning of health. Subjective measures are most conducive to emphasizing this. If a study of health in old age is concerned with the frequency of occurrence of certain kinds of health problems in some population, then more objective measures would be the most efficient techniques for collecting this information.

Is there a strong relationship between objective and subjective measures of health? If there is, this would lend support to the argument that health as an activity resource and changes in health status enter meaningfully into the personal behavior of old people. A strong relationship would also indicate that those processes that link objective states of health in individual contexts to personal meaning operate efficiently.

Overall, most studies have shown that there is a close relationship between objective and subjective measures of health. Self-ratings of health, however, generally tend to be more favorable in judgments of health than objective measures (Riley and Foner, 1968, p. 293). Comparing old people's ratings of their health with physicians' ratings, Suchman and his associates (1958) found that among 1000 males sixty-four years of age and older self-ratings of health were more favorable in either category of physicians' ratings of favorable or unfavorable. However, self-ratings did tend to be highest when physicians' ratings were favorable. Over time, self-ratings of health tend to be more stable than the objective measure of physicians' ratings. Data collected from 250 volunteer subjects, aged sixty to ninety-four, over the period of a few years showed that medical ratings of health declined over time while self-ratings remained more stable (Heyman and Jeffers, 1963).

In a comparative study, the data of which were drawn from representative samples of the aged populations of Denmark, Britain, and the United States, Shanas and others (1968) report that the relationship between objective and subjective evaluations of health is fairly strong. Self-ratings in each country were measured by respondents' answers to a question about their health which provided three possible responses—good, fair, or poor. Objective evaluation was measured by an "incapacity score," which is an index compiled from answers to questions about a respondent's capacity to perform six common tasks of daily life, such as going out-of-doors, walking up and down stairs, and dressing oneself. The relationship between these two measures of health in each country studied is such that Shanas reports:

> The old person's self-rating of his health is a guide to his degree of incapacity as measured by our index. For each country and for both sexes, the higher the incapacity score, the greater the proportion of old people who feel their health is poor (p. 56).

As in other studies, however, Shanas reports that her comparative data show that in the highest incapacity category, there are persons who still optimistically rate their health as "good."

> Interestingly enough, in all three countries there are a group of health optimists, persons with incapacity scores of 7 or more [range is 0 for best to 12] who think their health is good. . . . Some proportion of those with only minimal impairments (scores of zero to two on our scale) considered themselves to be in poor health and undoubtedly should be classified as health pessimists. In each country, however, optimism about health among the elderly is more usual than pessimism (p. 56).

Regardless of type of measure, whether objective or subjective, data on health for any particular sample of old people tend to be highly correlated. How then do these measures of health relate to the degree of behavior flexibility? Behavior flexibility has not been defined here as equivalent to active degree of behavior, but rather as the active *or* potential degree of behavior influenced by activity resources. Most studies of the relationship between health as a resource and flexibility have focused on active flexibility, or activity. Measures of potential flexibility, however, could be constructed through questions on hypothetical activities in which a respondent could or could not engage, as he saw it.

There is evidence that self-ratings of health are associated with quality and degree of activity. Old people who are actively involved in various kinds of social activities tend to rate their health higher than persons who are less involved, objective health being equal. Maddox (1962b) found that among 250 subjects studied in his North Carolina sample, active persons were more likely to rate their health high than the inactive. Kutner and others (1956) report a similar difference between persons not isolated and those who are isolated. They also found that self-ratings of health varied positively with socioeconomic ratings.

Shanas' (1968) comparative data in three countries further corroborate the relationship between health and activity. The more mobile an elderly person says that he is, the more likely he is to report his health as good. Among those persons who reported that they were housebound, over half in Denmark and the United States and about half in Britain said that their health is poor rather than fair or good. If an activity distinction is made on the basis of whether or not an old person is ambulatory, about 90 per cent of those who are ambulatory rate their health as fair to good, with about 60 per cent stating good in each country (p. 54).

Studies of the relationship between objective health and activity, not surprisingly, have shown that these two factors are positively associated. Scotch and Richardson (1966), in a study of 1500 war veterans, eighty years of age or older, found that when health is measured by frequency of contact with a physician and days hospitalized, and when activity is measured by such indexes as number of active roles (e.g. being a friend, neighbor, or worker), daily interaction, and monthly contacts with others, activity is higher among the healthier than those with poor health. Maddox and Eisdorfer (1962) report the same kind of relationship between health and activity for both objective and self-ratings of health.

In addition to studies of the relationship between health and activity in general, some research has been done on the impact of health on specific kinds of activity. These have ranged from church attendance to recreational activities.

Maves (1960) reports in his review of several studies of aging and religious behavior that decreased church attendance is associated with poor health. Hunter and Maurice (1963), in a study based on a sample of 150 old people over sixty-five collected in Grand Rapids, Michigan, further support this relationship between attendance and poor health.

Data also show that there is a positive association between state of health and friendship. Hunter and Maurice (1953) found that frequency of visiting with friends was greater among those old people who were in good rather than poor health. This was also true when state of health was defined as being housebound or not.

Household activities of various sorts are related to state of health. In a study conducted by Beyer and Woods cited in Riley (1968, p. 139) which is based on a sample of over 5000 OASDI beneficiaries in four urban areas in the United States, it was found that ability to take care of day-to-day household activities decreases with the number of health problems reported. This relationship, however, is not a strong one.

Health is also related to work attendance and retirement. Kossoris (1948), in a study based on a sample of 18,000 workers in varied occupations in 109 manufacturing plants across the United States, states that illness accounts for about one-third of the amount of time lost by men at their jobs. This is higher for aged workers. In a panel study of 2000 male workers aged sixty-four, Streib and Thompson (1957) report that old people who retire are generally less healthy than those of the same age who remain working. And, Palmore (1964) states that among persons retiring at age sixty-five and over, in his survey of OASDI beneficiaries, poor health is the reason for retiring given by a little over half of the self-employed and about 40 per cent of wage and salary workers.

Besides varied kinds of work tasks, health also affects leisure activities among the aged. A national recreation survey (cited in Riley and Foner, 1968, p. 530) in which 4000 persons of differing ages across the United States were sampled and interviewed, indicates that participation in varied kinds of outdoor recreation activities by the elderly is loosely associated with state of health. Taking vacations and travel of various sorts and distances are also associated with state of health (Riley and Foner, 1968, p. 532). Persons in poor health generally report that they do not know what to do with leisure time or that they just have too much of it. Shanas' (1968, p. 61) cross-national data indicate that regardless of country, old people who evaluate their health as poor are most likely to state that "time passes slowly." This relationship is more pronounced in the United States and Britain than in Denmark.

SOLVENCY AND FLEXIBILITY

Next to health as an activity resource, financial solvency has the greatest impact on behavior flexibility (activity) in old age. The impact of solvency on activity is to some extent independent of the factor of health. Where they are related, they affect each other in two ways. First, poor health may lead to declines in income because of the following kinds of problems: unavoidable retirement due to health, reduction in usable income due to costs of medicine and/or other uninsured medical bills, and the costs of possible aids utilized in lieu of the self-performance of services. Second, the reverse process of reductions in income leading to poor health also occurs in old age. Insolvency implies that some health problems tend to remain unattended until they become more severe than they would have if income were higher. Low income also means that the transportation necessary for availing oneself of medical services may be relatively high in cost.

The importance of noting the interrelationship between health and solvency in old age is that it has a strong influence on the emergence of a group of persons who are low in flexibility in a special way. For any age-group, there is likely to be some interrelationship between health and solvency. However, what mades the interdependence between these factors salient among the elderly are primarily two characteristics. One is that the combination of relatively severe problems or potential problems in *both* health and solvency is specific to old people. The second is that when either of these problems is encountered in old age it is more likely to be chronic than at a younger age. Certainly, being poor in income and/or health is not limited to the aged as a group. But, it is old people who as a group have the greatest chance of being extensively and chronically affected by changes both in health and income.

Although some degree of interdependence exists between the states of health and solvency for old people, this does not imply that the two resources are identical. They tend to vary together within limits.

The limits that exist for variations in each of the resources of health and solvency are social limitations which differ from country to country. In the United States, variations in the state of health are affected by different kinds of medical insurance and/or services available to the aged independent of income. Such health plans provide both a minimum degree of care for health problems as well as a ceiling on that which can be attended to under the plans. The same is true with income provided primarily by Social Security (OASDI) benefits or various kinds of private employee retirement plans. Depending on the length of employment history as well as kinds of income, persons in old age typically receive a minimum, relatively fixed income. Generally, such income has a ceiling which depends upon such factors as whether or not a spouse or potential spouse is receiving similar income or upon whether or not a person chooses to remain employed at an income level that precludes receiving federal and/or retirement income benefits.

Aside from the fact that health and solvency are treated as two different things by varied persons and agencies dealing with the aged, it is also the case that the aged themselves distinguish between the two. When asked about some of the problems that they themselves see as affecting their life satisfaction, they clearly distinguish income from state of health (Gubrium, 1971). It is not the case that all aged persons who are insolvent are also poor in health. In the Detroit Study, when both factors of health and solvency were measured objectively and subjectively, persons with different combinations of varied degrees of health and solvency were found.

Because of the foregoing relationships between health and solvency in old age, it is reasonable to isolate solvency as an activity resource having an independent impact on behavior flexibility. What are some of the facts that are known about the relationship between solvency and flexibility? Again, as in health and flexibility research, studies of the relationship between solvency and flexibility have usually defined flexibility in its active sense as activity tending to ignore what the aged see as the potential or the extent of activity in which they could engage if they so desired.

Activity in general is related to socioeconomic status. When activity is defined either in terms of being actively involved in the performance of a variety of adult roles or in terms of different sorts of recreational activities, most studies (Kutner *et al.*, 1956; Lowenthal, 1964; Maddox and Eisdorfer, 1962) have shown that persons who come from higher socioeconomic backgrounds than lower ones tend to be less isolated and more actively involved in their communities. Moreover, aside from the impact of socioeconomic status on activity, there is evidence that being employed per se in old age affects activity. Maddox and Eisdorfer (1962) found that in their study of 250 old persons, sixty to ninety-four years old, those who were employed at least part-time had higher rates of activity than those persons who were not.

As with studies of activity and health, the relationship between several specific forms of activity and solvency has been focused upon. Among these several specific activities, there has been a major interest in friendship. Rosow (1967), in a study of 1200 elderly persons in Cleveland residing in multi-unit housing with varying proportions of old people, states that persons were more likely to state that they have "good friends" if they were middle rather than working class individuals. Kutner and his associates (1956) support this with their New York City data in which they found that the aged were more likely to have friends and to visit them fairly often if they were in higher rather than lower income strata.

Although studies of the relationship between income and friendship (number as well as frequency of contact) have shown that these are positively associated, there is also evidence that among the friends that they do have, the poor have a higher proportion of friends and more frequent contacts with friends in their immediate neighborhoods than do those persons who have higher incomes. Rosenberg's (1970) study of working-class men and women in Philadelphia, aged forty-five to seventy-nine, shows evidence that those who were poor as opposed to solvent tended to be less isolated when their neighborhoods had relatively high concentrations of persons over forty-four years of age. Old people who are insolvent are most sensitive, in terms of friendship activity, to the age-composition of their neighborhoods. Langford (1962) also found that persons with low incomes were more likely than solvent old people to have most of their friends in their neighborhoods.

Overall, these findings tend to support the proposition that solvency is an activity resource as far as its influence on friendship formation and maintenance is concerned. Solvency also affects friendship indirectly in that it makes persons differentially sensitive to their social contexts. Those who are insolvent are more sensitive to the age-composition of their local neighborhoods than those who are more solvent.

The relationship between solvency and activity also emerges in various studies of the effect of retirement on old age. Shanas and others (1968), in their research on the behavior and attitudes of old people in Denmark, Britain, and the United States, focused on this question to some extent. One effect of retirement which they investigated is how retirement influences what persons feel about time and being alone. The employed in each country are more likely than the retired to say that "time never passes slowly." The retired are also less likely than the employed to say that they are "never alone," although for the United States the difference is almost nil.

In the same study, Shanas and others also asked respondents what items they missed in retirement. Among those cited, the following were the ones mentioned by most people: work itself, money, people at work, feeling of being useful, and things happening around one (p. 343). From this listing of major items missed, it is evident that persons do miss the activity of work and the active aspects of events connected with work. The relative emphases given to these different items varied from country to country as well as from one social class to another.

Although retirement may lead to a reduction of work and work-related activity, it does not necessarily imply a withdrawal or disengagement from all social relationships. For example, Rosenberg (1970) states that his Philadelphia data show that retirement may not have any bearing on reducing contacts with kin. If anything, retirement increases this kind of social engagement.

Retirement itself, as the loss of a work role, may not have as great an impact on activity as reductions in income although the two are by no means completely independent of each other. Streib (1965) found that for a group of males which he investigated, retirement as opposed to continued employment, did not more frequently lead to reduction of active participation in friendship roles and community activity. Maddox and Eisdorfer (1962) report that old people who are employed at least part-time as opposed to not employed at all are more likely to have higher overall activity levels.

On the whole, the evidence suggests that if retirement leads to relatively severe reductions in income, then activity decreases. If, however, retirement for a person is not accompanied by drastic changes in solvency, then activities in areas previously neglected because of the demands on time of being employed may even increase. Of course, the impact of retirement and/or reductions in solvency on increases or decreases in activity is contingent on what is locally available in the social context of an aged person. A reduction in income as an activity resource may have little impact on social involvement if being active takes very few resources, which would be the case if the facilities for being active were locally available.

Solvency also has an impact on political participation in old age. When political participation is measured by voting, it tends to be more extensive among aged persons with higher incomes. This, however, does not imply that retirement per se reduces participation in voting. Among all men not employed, almost three-fourths of those over sixty-five vote as compared with a little over half in the under sixty-five age category (Current Population Reports, 1965).

How does solvency affect membership in voluntary associations as an activity? Beyer and Woods (1963), in a study of 5000 OASDI beneficiaries in several urban locations across the United States, found that there is a very definite relationship between income and membership in one or more organizations. Among old people, sixty-five and over, with incomes under $1000, 30 per cent said that they belonged to one or more organizations. The percentage belonging to the same number of organizations increases by income category to the point where among persons with incomes of $5000 and over, 61 per cent belong to one or more organizations.

The impact of solvency on participation in voluntary associations has been corroborated cross-nationally as well as in rural areas. Hutchinson (1954) reports that among persons aged fifty-five and over in Australia, the proportion with associational memberships increases from 20 per cent of those in the lowest income category to 65 per cent of those in the highest. Taietz and Larson (1956) found the same kind of relationship between participation and socioeconomic status in rural New York.

One of the explanatory problems of many of the foregoing studies of the relationship between solvency and activity is that they fail to take into consideration the effect of the social context of aged persons and what it makes available to them in terms of activity opportunities. Although a rather consistent relationship between solvency and activity has been found in most studies, the simple cross-tabulation of variations in solvency and activity may be hiding the influence of context on activity. There is evidence (e.g. Blau, 1961; Rosenberg, 1970; Rosow, 1967) that social context is a crucial intervening factor in the impact of activity resources on flexibility. Depending on what it makes readily available, an old person's social context may serve as a substitute form of activity resource for him and thereby sustain his social involvements in spite of reductions in resources. It does not take much of an income, for instance, to participate in age-oriented associational life if it is available "in the neighborhood." Moreover, it is likely to be "in the neighborhood" if a neighborhood is comprised of a type of clientele that frequents such association.

SOCIAL SUPPORT AND FLEXIBILITY

In addition to health and solvency, another kind of resource which the aged as a group are more likely to lose than other age-groups is that of social support. Social support refers to the primary relationships between a person and others which are taken for granted in sustaining a certain life style or degree of activeness. Usually, social support results from having a living spouse, although it also may be an outcome of a long-term, intimate friendship or a close relationship with some relative.

Social support as an activity resource is not limited to an absolute level of support such as having a living spouse. Rather, what is crucial in its influence on behavior flexibility is its continuity. This means that regardless of the absolute level and/or kind of social support that an aged person possesses, if the support to which he has become accustomed decreases, his behavior flexibility is likely to decrease. In view of this, two major types of social support continuity are evident: (1) the continuity of having the long-term social support of a living spouse, and (2) continuity in not ever having had the social support of a living spouse. Aged persons with living spouses as well as the aged who are single (never married) maintain continuity and thereby have not lost this activity resource or experienced changes in its influence on behavior flexibility. Aged persons who have sustained the death of a spouse and those who have been divorced, both fairly recently, are individuals who have experienced relatively extensive forms of discontinuity in support. These persons would be expected to report the greatest reductions in behavior flexibility as far as the resource of social support is concerned.

As time passes away from an event which produced social support discontinuity in a person's life, he gradually becomes accustomed to a new level of support. For example, as the number of years increases since a person was widowed, his social support becomes similar to the support of single persons. One would expect the long-term widowed to be closer in behavior to single persons than to those recently widowed or recently divorced.

If a distinction is made between those aged persons with relatively continuous and those with relatively discontinuous kinds of social support, and if a significant form of social support is assumed to stem from the marriage relationship, then two states of support follow: being married or single, and being widowed or divorced. Being married or single means that, whatever absolute level of social support exists for a person, he has experienced and continues to experience continuity in it. Having become widowed or divorced, on the other hand (with the exception of long-term widowhood or divorce), means that an aged person who has experienced either has also experienced a discontinuity in a level of social support to which he has become accustomed and relatively dependent. Because of the preceding differences in continuity, we should expect that when asked about possible problems of everyday life and changes in ability to deal with them, the married and single respond by expressing few or minor changes in coping ability, while the widowed and divorced express more drastic changes and greater difficulty in coping with everyday problems.

In his study of the family life of a sample of British old people, Townsend (1957) found that being single was a special kind of resource to persons when they grow older. The single, whether male or female, had acquired a life style that tended to be highly self-reliant. Whether everyday life problems concerned household tasks, work, acquiring services, or whatever, single persons tended to have developed routines to cope with each. Those who said that they were lonely were likely to have recently experienced some kind of social loss. These persons had become desolated. Being desolate, however, is a result of social discontinuity, not long-term isolation. The recently widowed, in the foregoing sense, have become desolate, but are not necessarily isolated in that they may continue to maintain other kinds of social ties. It is desolation or discontinuity in support that is experienced as a loss of behavior flexibility. One becomes less able to cope with the contingencies of various everyday situations. As Townsend (1957) states:

> And the main conclusion of this analysis is that people saying they were lonely were nearly all people who had been deprived recently of the companionship of someone they loved. They were *desolates* and not necessarily *isolates*. They were isolated only in the sense that they had *become* isolated, relative to their previous situation (p. 178).

Jeremy Tunstall (1966), in another British study of old people, found that many single persons who were aged had life histories of self-reliance. Many of these persons, when asked about the reasons for why they remained single, indicated that they had had experiences in early life that necessitated delaying marriage. Some had been the younger of several siblings who had taken the task of caring for an aging and/or sickened parent. Others had not married after having lost fiances in the First World War.

Most simply stated that circumstances were such that they never came near to being married.

One thing that is fairly clear in the responses of single aged persons in Tunstall's study to questions about their life histories is that they have learned to rely on themselves for doing many tasks which are typically divided between the activities of persons married to each other. Single persons, then, if they remain so into old age, maintain continuity in social support and coping ability into late life. Being single, although it may be defined negatively to some extent in earlier life, becomes of distinct advantage in old age. The single aged themselves see this as an advantage. However, they do not usually attribute their present life styles to the fact of having been single alone:

> The single were also asked whether there were any compensations for staying single, such as being more independent. Only a quarter of those who answered thought there was none: the majority thought there were compensations—especially negative ones such as avoidance of an unhappy marriage. But there was little sign of a single state being viewed as a positive opportunity for a woman to pursue her own career and develop her own interests. None said it had been necessary to remain single to develop her full potentialities as a machine operator, or for that matter, as a schoolteacher. The others spoke of compensations rather than positive advantages (Tunstall, 1966, pp. 136-37).

The foregoing findings on the relationship between continuity or discontinuity in social support, on the one hand, and of coping ability, on the other, were further supported in the cross-national study of old age undertaken by Shanas and others (1968). Data from Denmark, Britain, and the United States show that feelings of loneliness were more directly linked with variations in social loss than to isolation per se. As Townsend (1968) states:

> The data tended to support the hypothesis that desolation rather than peer-contrasted isolation is the causal antecedent of loneliness (defined as the unwelcome feeling of lack or loss of companionship) and may also be more important than isolation in explaining the propensity to suicide in old age (p. 285).

Having experienced discontinuity in social support means that one has become deprived of coping ability relative to that existing before changes in major social ties. A desolate aged person's relationship with his social context changes. Since such a person no longer possesses the same ability to cope with everyday problems (such ability being significantly linked to the aid of a spouse), the same social context now places a relative burden on him. Any social context operates under the assumption that persons within it can cope with its everyday events. When they cannot, then such persons feel "lonely," or "low," or "desperate." It is not typical of social contexts to alter themselves to meet the needs of any person within them. If they do, it is usually a result of a plurality of inhabitants having changed or the outcome of planned changes.

In addition to the foregoing evidence on the relationship between continuity in social support and activity in general, there is some indication that social support continuity is related to changes in political activity. Gubrium (1972), in a study of the impact of discontinuity in social support on political interest and voting in old age, cross-tabulated responses of persons who were married or single and those who were widowed or divorced with political activity. Continuous social support was defined in terms of being married or single, while discontinuous support was defined as being either divorced or widowed. Since political activity varies with age, this latter factor was controlled in examining the relationship between social support continuity and political activity.

When asked whether or not they had voted in the last presidential election, although 75 per cent of all respondents said that they had voted, persons with continuous social support outvoted those individuals who had experienced discontinuity (chi-square significant at $p < .10$). When asked how much interest they had in politics, persons who were categorized as continuous expressed greater interest than those who were discontinuous (chi-square significant at $p < .05$). The last question put to respondents dealt with whether or not they felt that their current interest in political affairs differed from what it was when they were forty-five years old. Among the continuous, 15 per cent said they had "less interest now," 51.3 per cent said "about the same," and 33.8 per cent said "more now." The discontinuous were more likely to say that they had "less interest now" (33.3 per cent), 45 per cent said "about the same," and 21.7 per cent said that they now had more interest. Differences in perceived change were statistically significant (p<.01, chi-square).

In order to understand the process that transforms loss in social support into reductions in political activity, respondents were probed on how they accounted for changes in their voting and interests. Typically, these persons answered that they used to go to the voting polls with their spouse and that they usually discussed political candidates with him or her before voting. Many said that it was their spouse that used to keep their interest "up." Among the single, whatever level of interest in politics they had had in earlier life, they said was "pretty much the same now." Overall, most persons said simply that politics is not as interesting when you have no one with whom to discuss it or that it was "just not as easy to get up and vote with no one to go with like before."

SUMMARY

In this chapter, the meaning and characteristics of the individual context of an elderly person's environment have been delineated. Individual contexts influence persons insofar as they provide the means, and thereby also set the limits, by which persons cope with problems of everyday life. Activity resources provide each person with a specific degree of flexibility in the face of the events in everyday worlds.

The transformation of activity resources into meaningful influences on a person's action occurs by means of at least three processes. One of these is the impact on a person's sensitivity to self that emerges with relatively sharp life cycle changes in resources. Another process is not linked to a person's own experience but rather to the experience of others, which he experiences vicariously. This vicarious kind of experience may lead a person to anticipate changes in activity resources before they occur in his own life. As a result of this process of anticipation, a person may become prematurely anxious about his ability to cope with problems of everyday life in his social context. The anticipation of losses in activity resources may lead to a deliberate reduction of activity as a "precaution" against possible actual declines. The social psychology of this process comes very close to that of actual declines in resources. A third process is the awareness of one's flexibility that results from increasing difficulty in maintaining social interaction.

Three kinds of resources were isolated as important influences on coping ability, namely, health, solvency, and continuity in social support. Although there is some interrelationship among all of these factors, they are not identical. These three factors are not exhaustive of the number of resources which persons may possess as individuals. However, taken together, they are those particular factors that are typically of greatest importance in old age. If anything, specific variations in them are the characteristics that make old age socially and behaviorally distinct in many of its dimensions from other age categories.

Chapter V

THE SOCIAL PSYCHOLOGY OF CONTEXTS

In Chapters III and IV, we have delineated dimensions and problems of the two contexts of an aged person's environment—the social and individual. From a person's point of view, these contexts become what he can expect of himself as a potentially active individual and what others expect of him, respectively. For a person dealing with his everyday world, these two sources of influence on him enter significantly into how he perceives and judges himself as well as how he reacts to these judgments. This response to himself that is linked to his behavior as an individual and social being, is generally referred to as "morale" in gerontological literature.

One thing should be clearly noted at this point. The fact that differing combinations of activity resources and activity norms per se may have specific morale implications for persons does not imply that they may not work to alter either activity resources or their social contexts. "Persons" are understood here in the sense of active, constructive beings, i.e. they work to change the conditions of their personal life if they can and wish to do so. Once given, individual and social contexts do not strictly determine the probability of persons exhibiting a certain level of morale. Rather, personal actions being equal, individual and social contexts influence morale and life satisfaction in particular ways.

Certainly, individual and social contexts set limits on a person's coping ability. But, given some ability to cope, a person may have several alternatives available to him by which to alter his environment and its impact on him as a person. These range from altering his social context by ceasing to be oriented to it in any significant sense, to regaining social support by remarrying or constructing social relations that are supportive and/or confidential. In short, a person here is not defined completely in terms of the individual and social contexts in which he behaves, but rather is conceived as partially independent of these contexts.

PERSONS AND CONTEXTS

There is both theoretical advantage and disadvantage in separating persons from contexts. The advantages stem from having a working language to deal with the actions of persons that are independent of social and/or individual influences, on the one hand, and from being able to deal with the limits of personal acts and intended meanings, on the other. The disadvantage occurs in the loss of conceptual parsimony that could result from utilizing either contextual or personal conceptions alone. Since the major effort here is aimed at understanding the processes by which old people behave rather than verifying particular propositions, the advantages outweigh the loss in parsimony pursuant to separating persons from contexts.

Flexible and Fixed Limits

Given the conceptual separation of persons and contexts, one way by which to conceive of the relationship between them is through the idea of *limits*. Contexts may be said to set varying kinds of limits for old persons' actions, whether definitional, active, or both. Conversely, persons, in their deliberate actions, may actively work to reconstruct their everyday worlds and thereby alter the limits of environmental influence on themselves.

Two kinds of limitation in contexts are evident. One of these is *flexible* in the sense that contexts limit a person's actions if he does nothing to alter and reconstruct parts of his individual or social world. For example, the activity resource of social support may be altered in its impact on a person if such a person works to regain it when it is lost. Suppose that an elderly woman has suffered the death of her spouse, on whom she had depended for coping with various everyday problems or, for that matter, depended upon simply as a source of confidence. What kinds of action could she take to reduce the limitations on her ability to deal with everyday life stemming from her loss? For one thing, she might remarry. Or, she might develop a close friendship with another widow. The point is that *her* active decisions may alter environmental limitations on her ability to cope. Social contexts may also have flexible limitations, i.e. social limitations that exist only as long as persons choose to do nothing about them. For instance, suppose a person resides in some context that places a relatively extensive burden on old age in that local expectations of behavior are defined in terms of active, working, middle-adult life styles. In such social contexts, behavior expectations are difficult to fulfill if one is relatively highly susceptible to factors making for drastic reductions in activity, which is likely in old age and more so among some old people. An aged person in such a social context, if he has the means, may change his residence to one in which activity norms and behavior expectations are more closely aligned with his capabilities. Moreover, the matter of change may not be a question of having the means (e.g. economic capability), especially for moving into some age-concentrated contexts (type I), but rather a matter of choosing to change one's context and acting upon the choice made. By so choosing, an aged person changes social constraints on his actions and capabilities, thereby altering the social limitations on his behavior.

Contexts may also be *fixed* in the limits which they place on persons' actions. This is a more severe kind of limitation in that personal choice alone does not alter them. There are two ways in which limitations may be fixed for a person. These are the fixed limits of individual and social contexts.

Individually, the factor of growing poor health gradually decreases the flexibility of persons to act and thereby influences their coping ability in particular situations. Holding social context constant (e.g. focusing on persons in type IV social contexts), a person with good health is not hindered in his capacity to perform in line with expectations of behavior defined by local activity norms. Across varied types of social context, a person with the resource of satisfactory health has the capacity to cope with expectations ranging from the relatively variable and intense demands on behavior of type IV social contexts to the relatively stable and mild demands of type I contexts. Regardless of whether the question is one of coping ability in a single social context or across several, the state of a person's health is an individual limitation that is relatively fixed in its influence on him. If he is in good health, he can cope with the contingencies of a variety of social contexts. If he is in poor health, however, he is limited in his coping ability, personal efforts at improving coping ability usually being ineffective. Being a fixed rather than flexible limitation is largely a function of (1) the typically "irreversible" nature of health problems in old age, and (2) the demoralizing effect of chronic health experiences on a person's willingness to deal with them in some manner so as to partially overcome their limitations.

Insolvency also tends to be a relatively fixed limitation on coping ability. This limitation is not "irreversible" to the same extent as the problem of chronic health loss in old age, for it is more a social structural condition than is poor health. This, however, does not mean that, as far as the actions of a single person, the irreversibility of health problems is not similar to insolvency in its impact on coping ability.

In any social context, several intervening circumstances may alter the fixed limitations of health and/or solvency on a person's coping ability. These circumstances are not necessarily common to any one type of social context, nor for that matter, occur with any particular frequency in any of them. For example, given a specific social context—say type IV—if health and solvency are relatively poor for an individual, it should follow that coping ability for such a person is low. However, the problems of coping ability that would be expected on the basis of knowledge of health and solvency alone would not be observed if, for instance (1) an aged person were part of a circle of friends that function so as to extend his coping ability through their systematic aid to each other's efforts at resolving everyday problems including mutual encouragement and reassurance, or (2) an aged person were financially the ward of someone who was economically solvent.

Social contexts may also set fixed limitations on the actions of old persons, i.e. they may hinder persons' actions regardless of their efforts to overcome the limits. For instance, given a person with relatively poor health or income and no available associates on whom to depend as coping aids or as income substitutes, particular social contexts are likely to place relatively strict limits on his ability to deal with problems of everyday life. In type IV contexts, an old person with poor health and/or one who is insolvent is likely to be severely restricted in his ability to fulfill everyday needs. A type IV context is not especially oriented in its varied dimensions (such as the concerns of neighbors or local services offered) to old people. Moreover, an insolvent or unhealthy aged person can do little to alter the impact of such a locale on his everyday life. He must, in effect, suffer the relatively fixed limitations it places on him. If such social contexts change so that local age composition becomes more homogeneous (e.g. through neighborhood age transition), then over time (if other influences such as racial or ethnic transition and urban renewal remain constant) fixed social limitations on coping ability will tend to change. Local services are likely to reflect local population characteristics and demands. With age-specific services and potential friendships available, the ability of persons to cope with everyday needs becomes less of a problem.

Limitation Nets

The overall relationship between persons and the several kinds of contextual limitations imposed upon them may be conceived as *limitation nets*. If coping ability is that aspect of personal action that is considered the object of limitations, each kind of environmental limit added to any other may be said to decrease the chances of an old person's being able to deal effectively with varied problems of everyday life. Each limitation which is imposed "closes off" a source of abilities to cope, and along with it the chances to alter one's environment.

Differing kinds of limitation nets place persons in varied circumstances. There is no implication inferred here that limitation nets are increasingly restrictive in the kinds of circumstances in which they place the aged. It is possible that a sequence of environmental changes, individual and/or social, has developed so as to alter fixed limitations on personal coping ability by decreasing them. This was the case in the foregoing example of reductions in activity resources followed by changes in the age-concentration of a local social context. In this case, the coping ability of a person initially had been hindered by the fixed limitations imposed by growing poor health or insolvency, and subsequently was altered through a reduction in the scope of limitations resulting from neighborhood changes which led to increased age-homogeneity and the local service and friendship implications of such homogeneity.

The concept of limitation net is the socio-environmental analogue of the concept of human development. The developmental approach to persons conceives of coping ability as an ordered process which is a function of such varied psychological conditions as "maturing," "growing old," or simply "growth." Such change or maturation generally is thought of as a sequence of stages typifying "normal" human psychological processes over time. The stages are considered to be a "natural" sequence. The socio-environmental conception of limitation nets, in contrast to this, does not analytically restrict life cycle changes in coping ability to any "normal" or "natural" sequence. From a socio-environmental point of view, so-called stages of human behavior would be said to emerge with increases in the probability that most persons would experience similar life cycle, environmental influences in a highly sequential manner. The probability of events occurring at particular times might make for stage-like life cycles, but the logic of limitation nets does not itself infer such stages. Although the concept of limitation net may be analogous to the idea of developmental stages, it is not equivalent. The basic difference between them lies in the fact that one conceives of stages as typically or normally ordered, while the other does not.

Other Approaches to Limits

There are at least two other approaches to the concept of limits in sociological literature. These represent extreme positions on the concept rather than the moderate approach taken here. They are the functionalist approach (cf. Parsons, 1951) to limits and the approaches of the exchange theorists (cf. Homans, 1961) and ethnomethodologists (cf. Garfinkel, 1967; Dreitzel, 1970).

The functionalist approach pushes the fixity of limits to the point where a person's rational decisions become a pure function of systemic norms. The behavior of persons is referred to as "action." "Action" as utilized by the functionalists, especially Parsons, is not the same as the idea of action in the socio-environmental approach to aging. The action of the socio-environmental approach is more nearly Weberian (cf. Weber, 1947, pp. 112-115) than Parsonian (the middle Parsons) in the sense that action is, although socially meaningful, still defined as partially free of normative prescriptions.

Exchange and ethnomethodological approaches to behavior represent an opposite view of behavior limitations. Both stress the flexibility of limitations, the ethnomethodologists to the point where they state that there are no ongoing, fixed social prescriptions of behavior—everything is taken for granted or negotiable. From their point of view, behavior is the sum of individual persons' conducts and constructs. Although both exchange and ethnomethodological approaches tend to eschew fixity in behavior limitations, they do this differently, for the former has intellectual roots in economic-objective views of human behavior while the latter traces its roots to the linguistic-subjective concerns of symbolic interactionism and phenomenology.

The theoretical advantage of the functional, exchange, and ethnomethodological views over socio-environmentalism is that of parsimony. This becomes an empirical advantage in the analysis of *highly visible* forms of normatively well-prescribed and normatively committed action, on the one hand, or highly visible forms of calculated or socially-constructed acts, on the other. However, not all social acts are as visibly like either "pure" normatively well-prescribed acts or "pure" socially-constructed

ones. Some social acts and interactions readily appear to combine both, e.g. the social acts of old people with respect to their
individual and social contexts. In the latter instances, the socio-
environmental approach is a useful and efficient perspective from
which to examine the actions of elderly persons, social pressures
on them, the implications of each for self-regard, and their overall
views of their social world.

CONTEXT CONGRUENCY

From the socio-environmental point of view, both individual
and social contexts may affect morale and life satisfaction. Given
that persons do nothing to alter their environments, neither
individual nor social contexts, what predictions can be made
about morale on the basis of variations in context relationships
alone? It should be noted that in practice, several "intervening"
factors might serve to alter empirically the behavior that would
be expected based on these variations alone. From the socio-
environmental point of view, "intervening" factors of a personal
sort would depend on the fixity of limitations on specific persons.
If environmental limitations were relatively flexible, deviant
cases of morale would likely result which would not be due to
context relationships. As the fixity of environmental limitations
on persons increases, variations in persons' morale due to personal
coping efforts should diminish.

From the point of view of a person, his individual and social
contexts may be conceived as sources of expectations influencing
his behavior. With respect to himself as an individual possessing
a specific configuration of activity resources, a person expects a
degree of behavior flexibility, thereby believing that he has a
certain ability to cope with problems of everyday life. With
respect to his social context, a person knows that local others
have certain activity norms in mind that influence the overt
acts which they direct toward other persons about them. From a
person's point of view, the expectations of individual and social
contexts are (1) what he can expect of himself, and (2) what he
knows others expect of him, respectively.

The individual and social expectations of a person may be

either congruent or incongruent. The congruence of these expectations influences a person's satisfaction with his everyday life. Morale is also a function of the degree of congruence between such expectations, except that it is a state of satisfaction with the self.

Propositions made on the relationship between environmentally-linked expectations and a person's life satisfaction and morale assume that a person is behaviorally oriented to his activity resources as an individual, on the one hand, and local activity norms, on the other. If such orientations do not exist, a person would not take account of these mutually influential expectations in his actions. They would not enter into the judgments which he makes of himself as a person and of his everyday life. In short, they would be irrelevant to morale and life satisfaction.

Given personal orientation to both individual and social contexts, it will be assumed further that elderly persons feel most satisfied with themselves (morale) and their living conditions (life satisfaction) when there is congruence between what is expected of them by others of relevance and what they can expect of themselves (cf. Secord and Backman, 1961, 1965). Incongruence in these two sets of expectations will lead to low morale and life dissatisfaction.

If we focus on extreme forms of both individual and social contexts, their cross-classification yields four types of expectation congruency (see Fig. 3). The individual and social expectations of persons in types A and D environments are congruent. In type A, high resource persons face active adult behavior expectations. In type D, low resource persons face behavior expectations oriented to the elderly. We should expect persons to have comparatively high morale in both environments. The morale of persons in types B and C environments should be lower, but for different reasons. In type C, dissatisfaction results from a person's inability to perform as a "typically-defined" member of his social context. In such age-heterogeneous contexts, standard membership generally means possessing and/or exhibiting conduct typical of a variety of active or working adults. In type B environments, persons possess relatively high activity resources

SOCIAL CONTEXT

	AGE-HETEROGENEITY (ACTIVE ADULT EXPECTATIONS TYPE Ⅳ)	AGE-CONCENTRATION (AGE-LINKED EXPECTATIONS TYPE I)
HIGH RESOURCES	HIGH MORALE A	LOW MORALE B
LOW RESOURCES	LOW MORALE C	HIGH MORALE D

INDIVIDUAL CONTEXT

Figure 3. Types of expectation congruency.

and can expect a fairly high degree of activity from themselves. But, the incongruency here is an outcome of a person's individual expectations and potential activity being of a different degree and kind from that locally defined as normal. Age-concentrated contexts generally have extensive commitments to leisure and leisure activity. Moreover, there is evidence that instrumental or gainful activity is conceived negatively in them. Consequently, the kind of expectations that a high resource person has of himself in a type B environment is defined socially as relatively undesirable. Such a person, if he is significantly oriented to local others, becomes dissatisfied (exasperated) with himself, thus making for a state of low morale.

The foregoing propositions on the contextual relationships leading to high or low morale were founded on the assumption that persons feel uneasy or strained in incongruent social situations. This assumption has a rather close affinity with a fairly extensive tradition of similar approaches to persons' behaviors. These have been variously labeled "dissonance" (cf. Festinger, 1957), "congruity" (cf. Osgood and Tannenbaum, 1955), and "balance" (cf. Newcomb, 1953; Heider, 1946) approaches. Although the logic of these approaches to persons' conduct is similar, they differ in their behavioral emphases. For some, a congruency assumption underlies the relationship between attitudes in attitude organization. For others, the same assumption is taken to be the operating logic between persons' approaches to each other.

One very crucial behavioral condition is necessary for approaching conduct with the logic of consistency or congruency. This is that if the principle of congruency is to be operable, those entities which are said to be congruent or incongruent (whether attitudes or expectations) must be "simultaneously" relevant to a subject. For example, if the context of relevance for one attitude toward some object is independent of the context of relevance for an opposed attitude toward the same object, then the principle of congruency may not be operable. It is not difficult to feel highly negatively about something in one situation and differently in another without experiencing strain or being psychologically uncomfortable.

Because of this problem, it is necessary for congruency approaches to assume mutual relevance to a subject of behaviors said to be congruent or not. It was for this reason that our propositions on morale in old age, which were contingent on variations in the social and individual contexts of persons, assumed that social and individual contexts were behavioral orientations of persons.

CONTEXT CONGRUENCY AND FLEXIBILITY

How do persons respond to the strain of incongruent expectations and its effect on their morale? Under what conditions do they act so as to reduce strain? The question of persons acting upon the conditions making for strain would be meaningless if persons had been conceived solely as products of environmental influences (i.e. norms and resources). However, the socioenvironmental point of view considers persons and environments as partially independent of each other. Persons may *act* in response to the state of congruency in their environments. They may work to alter or cope with the inconsistent impact that their contexts have on their lives.

At this point, it is necessary to make another assumption— one about active human response to strain. Although it has been stated that persons grow dissatisfied with increases in strain upon their lives, it is being postulated further, that persons respond to dissatisfaction with tendencies to actively reduce strain or alter its sources. It should be expected, then, that not only will persons in types B and C environments (Fig. 3) feel dissatisfied with their lives but that they will *tend* to act so as to alter the sources of dissatisfaction, namely, some aspect of incongruent environmental contexts.

Although persons in incongruent environments may tend to act so as to reduce strain, this does not imply that such behavior will actually occur. The emergence of such acts will depend upon whether or not such persons *can* act, not on whether or not they would like to act. It has been assumed only that they tend to act so as to reduce strain. This brings our discussion back full circle to contextual limits on a person's coping ability.

In describing the relationship between persons and contexts as one of limits, it was said that such limits vary in terms of their flexibility. Some contextual conditions place limitations on person's acts by confining them to the effects of such contexts only if they do nothing to alter the contexts. Such limitations were said to be "flexible." "Fixed" limitations were those which constrained persons' actions notwithstanding their efforts to alter them.

Given that persons tend to act so as to alter incongruent environments, and that persons' attempts to alter them are differentially constrained by the degree of flexibility in limits imposed upon them, then a variety of active responses to the degree of congruency between contexts is conceivable. Taking flexibility in the limits imposed by contexts as one dimension and context congruency as a second, their cross-classification yields four types of active response (coping) to variations in context congruency (see Fig. 4), when each dimension is dichotomized into extremes.

Old people cope differently with varied states of context

CONTEXT FLEXIBILITY

		FIXED	FLEXIBLE
CONTEXT CONGRUENCY	**CONGRUENT**	HIGH MORALE NO ACTIVE ATTEMPTS TO ALTER CONTEXTS 1	HIGH MORALE NO ACTIVE ATTEMPTS TO ALTER CONTEXTS 2
	INCONGRUENT	LOW MORALE CANNOT ACT TO ALTER CONTEXT INCONGRUENCY 3	LOW MORALE (POTENTIAL HIGH MORALE) MAY ACT TO ALTER CONTEXT INCONGRUENCY 4

Figure 4. Types of active response to context congruency.

congruency depending upon two factors: (1) degree of morale associated with context congruency, and (2) the flexibility of contextual limitations. Among those with high morale (see Fig. 4), there is not likely to be any active attempt to alter environmental conditions, regardless of the flexibility of contexts. If persons are satisfied with their lives they should not make active attempts to alter them. This is indicated in cells 1 and 2 of Figure 4. Among persons with low morale (stemming from context incongruency), dissatisfaction with everyday life leads to a desire to alter conditions making for this state of mind. Persons with low morale tend to act so as to increase their life satisfaction. This potential active response among low morale persons is only a *tendency* as far as the dimension of context congruency.

Persons in incongruent environments will not necessarily be successful in changing their lives. Whether or not they actually make attempts and succeed will depend upon contextual constraints on their activeness. If these constraints are flexible, active responses may occur (cell 4, Fig. 4). If persons with low morale face fixed constraints, they remain the "captives" of circumstances (cell 3). Such elderly people suffer the dissatisfaction of negative self-judgments which is compounded by a personal inability to cope with and alter the conditions (individual or social) of everyday life making for dissatisfacton. Insofar as neither persons in type 3 nor 4 environments overtly act to alter sources of dissatisfaction (some not being able, others choosing not to exert the effort), they should continue to feel life dissatisfaction and exhibit low morale.

The Influence of Anticipation and Unique Roles

There was evidence in the Detroit interviews that a process of *anticipatory coping* may operate among some, but by no means all, old people in flexible-incongruent environments (cell 4, Fig. 4) resulting in relatively high morale in spite of apparent incongruency. The factor of anticipation is not a dimension of the typology outlined in Figure 4, but it may serve to discredit empirically what would be expected from the contingencies of the typology alone.

Although they would be expected to have morale as low as persons in fixed-incongruent environments (cell 3, Fig. 4), those persons in flexible incongruent environments (cell 4, Fig. 4) who (1) do not act so as to alter incongruency but (2) fully *anticipate* the possibility that they "could change things" if they wished and "just don't feel like bothering," exhibit less severe life dissatisfaction than others in the same environments (cell 4) who do not anticipate coping. This belief in what they might change if they desired among anticipatory persons in flexible-incongruent environments appears to be associated with a kind of blasé approach to altering everyday life (but not to everyday life per se). Such anticipatory persons were not found to be personally oriented to something other than local others in the Detroit Study. Therefore, they were still considered candidates for being included in the discussion of behavior in flexible-incongruent environments (cell 4).

What appeared to be typical of the few persons who seriously anticipated the possibility of altering their everyday lives was that none of them was at all eager or "excitable" about actively doing so. They knew that they possessed the ability to alter their everyday circumstances but stated clearly that "there's no real reason" why they should.

One such anticipatory person in the Detroit Study conceived of and presented himself as a benefactor to local others. As he would say, "I know that I'm better off than most of the people in this building." This man was in good health, a former public school teacher whose financial position was quite good as old people go, and he owned and drove a stationwagon. He often remarked that he knew that he "could afford something better and don't really have to live with people with problems like some here have." This statement, however, when it was made, was followed by ". . . but I get a kick out of helping others." He generally provided a reliable means of transportation for others in the same building when public transit was unattainable. He also made himself available as a source of physical help and readily offered assistance when it was requested. Such activity provided him with a steady source of life satisfaction which he defined as his "real obligation to others less fortunate." On the whole, it might be concluded that the few persons like this man interviewed in age-concentrated social contexts in Detroit direct their activity not at altering environmental incongruence but at being actively involved in local social life.

What locally sustains this kind of person is not that he is oriented in self-regard to some social context other than his immediate one, albeit this is one way that incongruency may be resolved, namely, by existing in a social context but not judging oneself by it. The social psychology of the foregoing subject as well as the few others like him did not operate in this way. Rather, in their local social contexts, others define them as "special persons." Although local behavior expectations are comparatively low in age-concentrated social contexts and often are bound with a subculture of aging, local others legitimize the necessity of "being different" for some persons in order to "provide help for those who can't do with their own problems." Because of the local public legitimation of activity for such persons, their social context and norms become congruent with their resources, approximating high resource–high activity norm environments.

The foregoing special case of a person with high morale in an ostensibly low morale-inducing environment, thus, is an outcome of two operating conditions. First, from the viewpoint of the person, the full awareness of his possible alteration of an incongruent environment reduces its effect on his morale. Second, local definitions specific to such a person legitimize his choice in deciding not to alter a potentially incongruent environment by uniquely constructing a congruent role for him.

It should be pointed out here that the above route to high morale among persons in flexible-incongruent environments (cell 4, Fig. 4) was exceptional rather than being typical. In the Detroit sample, persons who did not anticipate and chose not to alter incongruency when they could were typically dissatisfied with themselves and their life styles. For most of these persons, the route to life satisfaction through serious anticipation of a possible change in social context was simply not genuinely considered. They tended to brood and complain extensively, doing little to alter their environments. They appeared rather cynical, bitter, and somewhat sarcastic about local social life.

Fixed-Incongruent Environments

Persons in fixed-incongruent environments (cell 3, Fig. 4) are those who are likely to have the lowest morale. The conditions making for low morale in these environments do not allow persons to influence the impact which contexts have on their lives. Contextual conditions do not provide for the possibility of hopefulness, save of a spiritualistic sort. The morale of such persons is low—for many to the point of depression.

How do cell 3 persons conceive of their everyday circumstances? When asked what they might do to resolve some of the problems which they encounter in everyday life, their answers were typically expressed in a sorrowful, resigned manner. For some, this was followed by weeping. In the Detroit Study, it was surprising to find the extent to which such persons felt personally ineffective in influencing daily events. Many of their expressions of, "What can I do!" were said with feelings of resignation and some degree of fear. If anything, these persons felt "caught" in circumstances.

When the conditions of their individual or social worlds changed slightly, these changes had a further demoralizing impact on their lives and its routines. They feared alterations in their environments because there usually was no indication when they would occur, and moreover, they found it difficult to deal with them when they did occur. Slight changes in environments made for relatively extensive problems in adjustment.

The social context of these persons serves to constantly reinforce their state of low morale. They do not possess the resources which would allow them to cope easily with everyday problems and tasks typically encountered by individuals in age-heterogeneous contexts. The facilities of such contexts are structured specifically for persons with the resources of "active" working adults. Distances assume "traveling" ability. Quantities and types of goods sold locally assume solvency and a degree of demand often beyond that typical of the aged. The social interaction of local persons is often centered on non-local concerns such as work relationships. The conditions sustaining such non-local relationships for the non-aged do not usually sustain old people. These aged persons are, in short, in most ways tied to their local social context because their activity resources are poor. The social context of such old people, when it confronts them, constantly reinforces the unfulfillable demands that it makes on them. Their daily lives and the constraints on them are persistent reminders of their inability to cope.

The psychological state which emerges in many of these persons is resignation. This is not an outcome of simply accepting disengagement and voluntarily withdrawing from social life. Rather, such elderly persons know that they have little else to choose. As one woman notes, "It's not a matter of choosing—you can't do nothing, can you?" When these old people were asked about their future and what they wished for, one rather insightful gentleman captured the nature of responses quite well. He explained that, "I could wish for this or that—I know that—

but why be foolish?" When the anticipation of events to come was probed, it was of an entirely different character from that of anticipation among some old people in flexible-incongruent situations. It was not hopeful. It had no reason to be. When hopefulness was expressed, it was usually expressly noted to be "wishful thinking" (as one woman put it, "I'd be dreaming") or other-worldly. Regardless of whether it is the present or future, old people in fixed-incongruent environments consider the contingencies of their lives with unusual awareness and with resignation. As with many cases of being "caught" in situations, they seem to have thought extensively about them as well as thought harshly and realistically.

THE SOCIAL PSYCHOLOGY OF SOCIAL CONTEXTS

This chapter has shown (1) how the congruence of expectations associated wtih social and individual contexts affects morale, and (2) how persons respond to their contexts as a function of the degree of flexibility in constraints which contexts place on their action. The discussion of these topics centered on persons and the relationship between two contexts as they impinge on their everyday lives. Thus, so far, our focus on the social psychology of contexts has been person-centered.

There is another way to approach the social psychology of contexts. Its concerns do not focus on the person as such but rather on the social interaction among persons in varied social contexts. It is, of course, difficult to delineate explicitly the empirical differences between these two social psychological concerns. The difference tends to be one of emphasis and viewpoint. The first considers the operation of action from the viewpoint of the person within a social situation, while the latter approaches the actions of and interactions between persons from the point of view of the context or situation of action. The typology of social contexts outlined in Chapter III (see Fig. 2) can serve as a framework for the examination of the social psychology of *social* contexts. We shall limit our discussion to the social psychology of victimization.

Social Contexts and Extent of Victimization

One event which may occur in any type of social context in which old people reside is being criminally victimized. There is some evidence from the Detroit Study that the likelihood of being affected by such an event is partially dependent on the physical and social contingencies of different social contexts. How is it, then, that varied social contexts affect the behavior of persons within them as far as (1) extent of victimization, (2) beliefs about being criminally victimized, and (3) fear of crime?

Although the frequency of crimes committed against the elderly may not be as great as those committed against other age-groups (Ennis, 1967, pp. 34-35), the aged are more likely to suffer chronically as an outcome of those crimes of which they are victims. The aged as a group do not possess the physical agility, the financial resources, or the social support that allows them to recover as quickly or completely from criminal acts against them as other age-groups. Among old people themselves, however, those in the best of health who are financially solvent and who maintain supportive relationships are the least likely to respond chronically to victimization. These latter elderly persons most nearly approximate the responses of other age-groups to crime.

Given comparable individual resources, do certain types of social context influence the likelihood of being a victim of criminal acts in old age? For example, if extreme forms of age-concentration in social contexts are focused upon (types I and IV contexts; see Fig. 2), is it the case that old persons (with individual activity resources constant) differ in their chances of being victimized depending upon whether they reside in age-concentrated (type I) or age-heterogeneous (type IV) contexts?

Evidence collected in Detroit suggests that age-concentrated as opposed to age-heterogeneous social contexts are less likely to be the locale of crimes committed against old people or their property. Since the evidence for this is relatively scant and somewhat impressionistic, this discussion of criminal victimization and its relationship to old age social contexts is partially speculative in nature. The purpose served by such speculation is hypothesis-generation.

The evidence from the Detroit interviews is of two kinds. First, when elderly persons were asked about whether they had experienced any burglaries, robberies, or assaults, those in age-concentrated contexts tended to indicate less readily that they had had such experiences. Second, when respondents were probed further on what they thought was the reason that they or others like them had been victimized, most indicated that the reason was largely that "you just have to go out in the streets to conduct your daily business" and "that's where it happens," or when "you leave your house alone, they get in and rob." These kinds of explanations were most obvious among persons located in age-heterogeneous contexts.

Differential reports of being victimized between age-concentrated and age-heterogeneous contexts is evidence that may be questioned on at least two grounds when nothing else about the conditions of data-collection is known but that interviews were conducted in social contexts with different degrees of age-concentration. Two hypotheses rival that of differential social contexts as possible explanations for variations in victimization. If the age-concentrated as opposed age-heterogeneous contexts were located in areas of the city with low crime rates, then such rates may account for variations in the likelihood of being victimized. Another rival explanation would be that persons who come to reside in age-concentrated contexts have been lower life-cycle victims of crime than those who remain or come to reside in age-heterogeneous ones. In this second rival explanation, differential reports of having been victimized would not be a function of present social context but rather of the life span experiences of persons.

The Detroit interviews were conducted in such a way that there is reason to believe that these two rival hypotheses are not explanations of the differential victimization found. The design of the Detroit Study was constructed to tap the morale effects of variations in social context. In order to isolate the affects of local social contexts, other wider social contextual variables had to be controlled, e.g. such varying urban area characteristics as differential crime rates, age of neighborhood, transport facilities, and racial or ethnic composition. In order to control for these possibly confounding factors, different types of social context were sampled that were physically adjacent to each other. For example, when an age-concentrated high-rise residence (type I) was sampled, so was a mixed-age neighborhood (type IV) in the same vicinity. Because of this sampling format, there is reason to believe that variation in area crime rates is not a rival of social context as an explanation of differential victimization.

In the process of interviewing, it was realized that when respondents reported their victimization experiences, they were sometimes citing experiences as of five or ten years ago. It was known that some of these same respondents did not even reside in their present social contexts at that time. Because interest centered upon the effects of age-concentration versus age-heterogeneity on the likelihood of being victimized, the manner in which victimization experiences were being elicited had to be altered. It was then decided that persons would be asked whether they had been victimized in the last year. This minimized reporting of life span victimization experiences. This change in interview strategy lowered the importance of life span victimization as a rival of social context as an explanation of differences in the frequency of victimization between age-concentrated and age-heterogeneous contexts.

Although the two foregoing precautions were taken against rival explanations, it is still difficult to say that contextual differences in frequency of victimization can be taken as conclusive. First, a systematic record of differential victimization was not kept until about a fourth of the way through the interviewing. Second, some of the difference which appears may have been a result of the time-span that the original question on victimization experiences was tapping. The time-span of this question was altered shortly after a systematic record of victimization reports was begun.

The major reason why the scanty available evidence is not dismissed is a result of the probing that followed the question on victimization experiences. Following this item, respondents were asked to what they attributed victimization and whether they thought where one lived made a difference. Most persons noted that the cause was largely a matter of *protectiveness*. The features of certain kinds of living conditions are such that they protect the elderly from accessibility to criminals.

If they resided in age-concentrated contexts (type I), respondents would often say that much of what they need they can get "in the building." And, for business affairs which they must conduct outside of their buildings, services such as special transportation are often available. Aside from services that are specifically attached to the residences, the fact that such persons are age-concentrated makes local market demands for "age-oriented" products fairly high. This means that, aside from the formal residential "protectiveness" of age-concentrated contexts, the condition of age-concentration itself makes for a kind of protectiveness in that the daily needs of the aged become locally satisfiable. This unwitting outcome of age-concentration is not trivial. With age-concentration, a host of age-oriented facilities is likely to respond to local demands. These range from products for old people packaged in desired quantities to services of interest to them, such as transportation and income-maintenance information.

Those old persons who resided in age-heterogeneous contexts (type IV) were also probed on the conditions which they thought made for the victimization of the aged and whether the place where one lived might affect this or not. The kinds of conditions cited by these people contrasted with those mentioned by the aged in age-concentrated contexts. Conditions referred to ranged from neighborhood problems, to having to walk in "the streets" to reach various destinations, being afraid for one's possessions as a result of having to "leave the house unattended," and the lack of protection for old people. The absence of protectiveness and local age-oriented services makes it necessary for the aged to expose themselves to non-local social conditions. High exposure means that "ease of accessibility" to criminal actions is likely to be high.

Although both persons in age-concentrated and age-heterogeneous contexts said that where one lived did affect the chances of being victimized, the kinds of examples mentioned differed between the two contexts. Those in age-concentrated contexts typically cited the advantages of the existing protectiveness of their local residences. They would mention such things as "the building being locked," "the building superintendent is helpful in protecting residents from undue annoyances from outsiders," and the fact that they can lock their own doors or were "too high off the ground for anyone to break in." Persons in age-heterogeneous contexts, however, typically "wished for" the same kind of protectiveness as their age-concentrated counterparts. They wished that they could feel safe, that they could leave their homes "with some peace of mind," or that services which they needed would be closer and more convenient. Many of these persons said that they would sometimes do without needed items because the "streets didn't look that safe today." Several wished that their neighbors were home more often. Some said, however, that since the neighbors worked, it was of "little use to think of anyone around to watch out for you or your house when you were out."

One thing that was quite apparent among respondents in type IV contexts, which persons in age-concentrated contexts did not have as a disadvantage, was the lack of mutual aid among neighbors. Persons in age-concentrated contexts "looked out" for each other, as they would say. Neighbors would "check on each other" daily and this made them feel safer. They would "keep an eye" on each other's possessions when possessions had to be left unattended. Those in age-heterogeneous contexts, on the contrary, feared their local social worlds more. This fear was usually linked with expressed feelings of a lack of protectiveness in their surroundings and of being isolated. In the Detroit Study, some of the remarks of respondents in age-heterogeneous contexts were:

> Take fears—who hasn't got fears at what's happening. Everything is in such a turmoil. Like I said before, what's the use of bringing children into the world. Nobody seems to know what to do. It's all mixed up! You can't even step out. I'm not worrying about my future. Why should I? It wouldn't do any good!
>
> They broke into my house twice. The real estate people call sometimes twice a day and tell me that I should sell now. We can't even keep the windows open in the hot nights.
>
> I worry in case I take sick and die and be by myelf. [weeps] There's lot of things I'm afraid of. I'm afraid of someone breakin'

in and killin' me. Or, if I could be dead a whole week and no one would know. [weeps]

The foregoing evidence on the impact of age-concentration and its correlates on victimization suggests the following hypothesis:

> *Increasing age-concentration in social contexts tends to decrease the vulnerability of aged residents to criminal victimization because of concomitant increases in local protectiveness.*

Individual Resources and Extent of Victimization

Is there any indication that particular kinds of persons within each type of social context may be more vulnerable to being victimized than others? Again, the evidence from the Detroit Study is by no means conclusive, but the data which were collected suggest that persons with different kinds of individual resources are more vulnerable in some social contexts than others. Let us assume that, holding rate of local crime constant, the likelihood of being victimized varies directly with personal visibility. In age-heterogeneous contexts (type IV), persons with poor individual resources are likely to be the most visible. Such persons must walk, often slowly and haltingly, to their destinations. Their lack of social support and physical health make them easy targets because they are not likely to be aided in the prevention of victimization or to be very alert to possible sources of local crime. The poor resource individuals in age-heterogeneous contexts are more likely to react chronically when they are victimized than those with relatively extensive resources. In short, those old people in the least "protective" situations who can least afford being victimized are most adversely affected by crime both in terms of the likelihood of its occurrence as well as after it is committed.

If the visibility assumption holds, then again in age-concentrated social contexts (type I), the most visible elderly should be those persons most vulnerable to criminal victimization. In these contexts, many services are locally available and there is relatively extensive local protectiveness. Here, it is persons who possess the greatest activity resources who are the most visible. They most frequently leave the protectiveness of their contexts for various reasons, an important one of which is the fact that leaving is not difficult for them. Their relatively high mobility makes them most visible as potential victims.

On the basis of the foregoing argument and the evidence from the Detroit Study, the following three hypotheses are suggested:

> *Social contexts differentially affect old persons with varying activity resources in terms of vulnerability to being victimized.*
>
> *In age-concentrated contexts (type I), high-resource aged persons are most vulnerable to being victimized.*
>
> *In age-heterogeneous contexts (type IV), low-resource aged persons are most vulnerable to being victimized.*

Social Contexts and Beliefs About Crime

There is another aspect to the impact that different degrees of age-concentration have on victimization, namely, the influence that social contexts have on the *beliefs* of old people about the extent of crime. Although actual victimization was hypothesized to be higher in age-heterogeneous as opposed to age-concentrated contexts, this does not mean that beliefs about victimization vary in the same manner.

Beliefs about crime are contingent on the conditions that perpetuate the diffusion of information in social contexts. Although increasing age-concentration has been hypothesized as increasing protectiveness in social contexts which in turn serves to minimize victimization, the same increasing age-concentration enhances the diffusion-potential for any beliefs about crime. In age-concentrated contexts, communication between persons is likely to be more intense than in age-heterogeneous contexts because (1) they contain socially similar persons, and (2) these persons are proximate, which affects the chances of similar types of persons encountering each other. Because of these contextual factors, any beliefs about crime are likely to be more common and shared among the aged in age-concentrated contexts than in age-heterogeneous ones.

The information-diffusion contingencies of age-concentrated contexts make it highly likely that a "belief-magnifying effect" will occur in them. In addition to the likelihood that beliefs about crime are similar, each person's belief is also continually corroborated by others' similar beliefs because of the relatively frequent encounters between persons. This tends to magnify a set of common beliefs, reinforcing them through each person's acceptance and subsequent communication of them. In effect, each person has beliefs about crime and is continually informed about the same beliefs by immediate others.

The local conditions making for and perpetuating common beliefs about crime in age-concentrated social contexts are minimized in age-heterogeneous contexts. What each person believes about the state of crime in age-heterogeneous contexts is likely to be more variable than in their age-concentrated counterparts. There are persons, e.g. young adults and adolescents, whose concern with possible crime may be comparatively minimal. There are others, e.g. working adults, whose resources and everyday activity make much of their daily life non-local. Consequently, the social types living in age-heterogeneous contexts are not as likely to have common interests and common daily experiences as persons in age-concentrated contexts. Encounters between differing social types in age-heterogeneous contexts are not likely to occur as often as between similarly aged persons in age-concentrated contexts. Because of this, any beliefs which may be shared by the aged and younger adults in age-heterogeneous contexts are not reinforced through communication.

The following hypothesis on the social psychology of victimization beliefs follows from this argument:

> *Beliefs about being criminally victimized are more common and magnified among old people in age-concentrated social contexts than among those in age-heterogeneous ones.*

In addition to the protectiveness of social contexts and its effect on victimization, victimization beliefs may also influence the extent of victimization. If victimization beliefs in age-concentrated contexts are indeed more extensive than in age-heterogeneous contexts, such beliefs may serve as a source of continual cautioning about crime to elderly persons in the former contexts, thereby potentially leading them to take precautions against being victimized. Both protectiveness and greater precaution may then make for less actual victimization in age-concentrated contexts than in age-heterogeneous ones.

In the Detroit Study, belief systems constructed around victimization were found and appeared to be most prevalent in age-concentrated contexts. When persons in these contexts were probed on their experiences with crime in the last year, although many could not cite specific experiences which they had personally undergone, there certainly was no dearth of references to specific cases of victimization "in the building." What was rather surprising was that these same cases were consistently and continually cited as evidence of the extent of crime committed locally. This collective citing of cases was not limited to named instances of local victims, but there also was remarkable consistency in the details cited about unnamed instances of victimization.

When aged respondents in age-heterogeneous contexts reported on their beliefs about the extent of local crime, their statements were highly variable. They varied in two ways especially: (1) there were differences in what was believed about victimization, some persons believing local crime rates to be fairly high, others reporting that their neighborhoods were relatively safe; and (2) what appeared to be common references to examples of local crime generally were not shared in as great detail as the common references of persons in age-concentrated contexts.

The impact of age-concentration on beliefs appears to operate in such a way as to minimize the range of what is believed locally. As local social similiarity increases, the range of local beliefs tends to decrease. This process leads to the development of a common system of beliefs. In age-concentrated social contexts, victimization "awareness" is likely to emerge, i.e. collective awareness of a set of beliefs about being victimized. On a more general level, Rose (1965a) has referred to this phenomenon as a growing "group consciousness" among old people leading to a "subculture of aging." In the area of behavior being discussed here, this emergent common body of beliefs among age-concentrated old people might be referred to as an emergent "subculture of victimization."

Responses to Beliefs About Victimization

We have noted above that there is some reason to believe there are differing proportions of victimization and kinds of victimization beliefs in age-concentrated as opposed to age-heterogeneous contexts. How do persons respond to victimization beliefs and do these responses vary from one social context to another?

Persons interviewed in Detroit were asked how they felt (how did this make them feel) about what they believed to be the state of crime in their social contexts. A comparison of the evidence that is available from differing social contexts indicates that personal responses to beliefs about crime may vary from one social context to another.

Aged respondents in age-heterogeneous contexts varied relatively widely in their range of beliefs about crime in their neighborhoods. When asked how they felt about this (beliefs about crime), those who believed crime to be extensive said that they feared for their safety. Such answers as being "afraid to go out," or being "afraid for my things," or "my house" were typical. They reported that they were generally fearful of their neighborhood and that this made them nervous.

Persons in age-concentrated contexts responded differently to questions on how they felt about what they believed the state of crime to be. They did not mention as frequently that crime made them fearful, anxious, or nervous. Their responses, rather, were more typically externalized than those of their age-heterogeneous counterparts. Persons in age-concentrated contexts said that they felt "more police protection" was necessary, that "they should punish criminals more than they do," or that "life has just become more rotten and should be changed." Although there certainly was variation in feelings expressed, many persons referred to some feeling about an object other than the self. Responses in age-concentrated contexts were typically made in a tone of anger rather than fear.

What may make for differences in response between old people in age-concentrated and age-heterogeneous contexts is the same condition that makes for differences in victimization belief-coalescence and magnification, namely, the varied structure of encounters and interaction in social contexts. Because the encounters and interaction between old persons in age-concentrated contexts are relatively frequent and intense, it is not as easy for persons in them to respond to victimization beliefs individually as it is in age-heterogeneous contexts. Responses in age-concentrated contexts are likely to be shared reactions to a commonly defined condition. Shared responses are a more external kind of reaction than the responses of isolated old persons in age-heterogeneous contexts. Among the latter, the relative lack of common and shared beliefs about victimization makes for isolated reactions to the beliefs that exist in each person's mind.

The foregoing discussion of the relationship between social contexts and responses to beliefs about victimization suggests the following hypothesis:

> *Old people in age-heterogeneous social contexts are likely to respond to victimization beliefs with fear, while those in age-concentrated contexts are more likely to respond with anger.*

Chapter VI

GROUP-CONSCIOUSNESS AND AGE-CONCENTRATION

THE TERM *group-consciousness* refers to an awareness in a collection of persons of some common condition of their lives that is of interest to them as a group. The distinguishing characteristics of being group-conscious are threefold: (1) persons involved must be subjectively aware of some common interest among them, (2) the awareness must be shared among members of the group, and (3) the objects of awareness are located within the group's experience. It is not sufficient that the aged be simply an objective interest group. The actions of old people as group-conscious actions necessitate their being subjectively aware of their common interests. Group-conscious actions also necessitate social interaction among a collection of persons. This means that relative proximity is important in the development of group-consciousness.

Even though age-concentration may not lead automatically to group-consciousness among old people, it nevertheless provides two of the conditions necessary for its emergence, namely, it maximizes the shared experiences of a collection of persons and facilitates interaction among them. Whether or not age-concentrated old people become subjectively conscious of their group interests is a function of at least two other factors: (1) the relationship of the group to outsiders, and (2) sources of influence within the group, e.g. leadership of various kinds.

In the foregoing chapters, several instances of group-consciousness have been noted within age-concentrated social contexts in Detroit. For example, old persons in age-concentrated social contexts are aware of behavior expectations that are relatively highly age-linked. They expect age-linked kinds of activity from immediate others and expect immediate others to expect the same of themselves. Another example of group-consciousness was noted in the discussion of beliefs and feelings about crime and victimization in old age. When asked what they believe to be the state of crime currently, persons in age-concentrated contexts are comparatively unanimous and consistent in what they believe. There also is some indication that they express a common anger about the state of crime, which is reinforced in daily social interaction.

AN APPROACH TO GROUP-CONSCIOUSNESS IN OLD AGE

In examining evidence in the gerontological literature on the factors which influence the emergence of age-awareness and group-consciousness among the elderly, a distinction is being made between external and internal factors. Those which have a source in behavior outside the collection of old people are referred to as external factors. Those having a source in the behavior of the elderly are referred to as internal factors. This is a useful distinction to make since these two kinds of factors are relatively independent of each other and independently influence age-awareness and group-consciousness.

External factors are located in the behavior of non-aged persons toward old people. This refers both to active influences on old people involving overt actions and to beliefs and feelings of the non-aged about old people which are verbally expressed and perpetuated.

Internal factors are located in the relationships between aged persons themselves and how the nature of such relationships affects their awareness of themselves as a distinct collection of persons. The operation of such internal influences on group-consciousness is partially dependent on age-concentration, which in turn is dependent on proximity and age-homogeneity.

Given that the foregoing two types of factors have an impact on the emergence of group-consciousness in old age, what collective state of the aged does each influence? External factors may influence old people either as a collectivity or as a group. A collectivity is a set of persons with some publicly-defined common characteristic, but among whom there is little or no social interaction that is sustained over time. A group is a collectivity of persons in which social interaction is sustained over time. Internal factors, in contrast to external ones, necessitate some degree of sustained social interaction among persons in order to be operable, for these factors are influences on persons by the same persons. Because of this, the collective state influenced by internal factors is one that is group-like.

In addition to the distinctions made between internal and external factors, on the one hand, and collections and groups of elderly persons, on the other, a third distinction is made between age-awareness and group-consciousness. These latter two are being referred to as stages of awareness of being old.

Age-awareness is the knowledge of a collection of elderly persons that each of them is being socially delineated in terms of age. Being age-aware means that a person realizes that his age will lead to age-distinctions in his relationships with others. This implies that self-references also will take age-distinctions into account. A collection of old persons becomes age-aware to a great extent as a result of the behavior of the non-aged in labeling them as a distinct set of persons (cf. Becker, 1963). Being age-aware does not imply that a collection of persons necessarily shares a common sense of destiny. Each member may be aware of the collection labeled old people and have personal evaluations of age-distinctions, but at this stage, each does not actively share and/or act upon the social implications of age-distinctions with other aged persons.

The second stage of awareness of being old refers to the internal reaction of a group of old people to age-distinctions. When this occurs, age-awareness has developed into group-consciousness. The factors making for this development are endemic to the increasing age-concentration and social interaction among the elderly. A group of persons that is aware of its distinctive characteristics constructs a common approach to itself and routinizes a language of age-distinction. Age-oriented behavior and expectations become part of an everyday way of living. In sharing common experiences in the face of age-discrimination, the development of a consciousness of shared interests is a short step away.

The Emergence of Group-consciousness

The foregoing discussion has outlined in brief the nature of relatively distinct aspects of the emergence of group-consciousness among the aged. Given these distinctions, what is the process of emergence suggested by evidence currently available? Saving a more detailed discussion of evidence for the following sections, what appear to be the overall dynamics of emergent group-consciousness among the aged?

Figure 5 schematizes both the distinctions discussed above and the process of emerging group-consciousness among old people suggested by existing evidence. The development of group-consciousness is conceived as a process of emergence which results from the interaction between aged and non-aged persons. It is, therefore, not solely a "natural history" approach to the emergence of group-consciousness. The logic of the natural history approach is, in overall strategy, quite similar to develop-

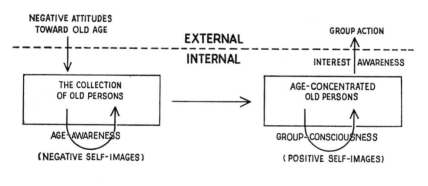

Figure 5.   Process of emergent group-consciousness in old age.

mental logic, save the fact that the terminology of the former has been most utilized by sociologists while developmental terms more typically have been used in psychological circles.

A natural history of emergent group-consciousness in old age would tend to de-emphasize the interrelationship between "contestants," i.e. the interrelationship between a collection or group of old people and the general public. The focus of the natural history approach is on the social development of a group of persons per se as it changes over time. This means that the natural history of old people as an emergent interest group, or as a variety of interest groups focused on specific age-issues in particular locations, would be traced with attempts to describe relatively distinct stages of development. The natural history approach does not limit itself to outlining the stages of any particular movement. It typically proceeds beyond this, generalizing to what might be the natural stages of any movement growing in group-consciousness.

Because the natural history approach centers attention on the group as a developing entity, it tends to ignore the conditions that make for movement from one stage of development to the next. One explanatory problem of ignoring these conditions is that the approach may readily dismiss the question of future movement developments by stating that "the next stage will emerge." Stating that "it will" is not nearly as informative or interesting as stating the conditions under which "it will," thereby making for an understanding that is somewhat closer to prediction than imminence.

As Figure 5 indicates, whether or not the two stages stipulated emerge depends on contingencies both external and internal to a set of old people. Any conceivable set of persons is not reacted to by others until it has been meaningfully delineated. If this were not the case, there should be no reason why spans of any number of years should not each be behaviorally relevant. Since this does not occur, some form of socially meaningful delineation of a set of persons must be made in order for such persons to emerge as a behaviorally distinct collection. For the set of aged people, the generally negative attitudes and actions toward them that differs markedly from any similar treatment of other age categories has delineated that particular age-span as a socially distinct collection of persons.

If only a socially-meaningful distinction of age is made without any pejorative connotation, what is commonly known behaviorally as a minority group does not emerge. A set of persons that is socially and meaningfully delineated may be publicly valued or devalued. It is only when the delineation of a particular collection of persons is devalued that it is acted toward, and itself acts like a minority group. In the United States, at least, there is evidence that the aged are thought of as a special collection of persons, and furthermore, are devalued as a collection (cf. Palmore, 1969, pp. 47-55). Thus, there is reason to believe that the aged in the United States, as a collection, have become a minority group (see stage I, Fig. 5).

Palmore and Whittington (1971) have noted recently that there has been some debate in the last ten years over whether the aged in fact are a minority group. This debate has revolved to some extent around various definitions of what constitutes a minority group. Streib (1965a) has argued that the aged are not a minority group, his position being a result of identifying minority group wth group-identity and group-consciousness. Rose and Peterson (1965) and Palmore (1969) have taken the opposite position in stating that the aged do constitute a minority group because of prevalent negative attitudes about old people and discrimination against them.

In the approach to emergent group-consciousness being outlined here, the conception of a minority group does not include the qualification of being an active interest group or being group-conscious. Rather, if a collection of persons has been socially delineated and devalued, this collection will be said to constitute a minority group. Stage I in the process of emergent group-consciousness is the stage of social delineation and devaluation.

It is not safe to identify a socially-delineated and devalued collection of persons, by that fact alone, as an interest group. The reason for this is that being an interest group, especially an active one, assumes some degree of organization among a collection of persons, i.e. it assumes that the collection is acting like a group rather than as individuals. However, a collection of old people may constitute a minority group in terms of social delineation and devaluation without being conscious of their internal ties or interacting with each other as a group. The responses of a collection of old people to the negative delineations of others, insofar as they remain a collection or minority group, are "quiescent" responses, i.e. responses are characterized by self-avoidance and self-degradations rather than group action. Persons constituting a minority group are aware of their negatively defined status, but are not necessarily highly overt or verbal about it. The conditions (one of which is age-concentration) which make for the emergence of, and behavior characteristic of what will be referred to as stage II are not prerequisites to the emergence of minority group behavior.

Given that the conditions for the emergence of stage I are operating, i.e. that old age has been socially delineated and is devalued, what impact does negative delineation have on the collection of old people? Specifically, how do elderly persons respond to these negative evaluations?

Since age-concentration is one of the factors that leads to the transformation of old age minority behavior into interest group action, minority group behavior should be most evident in age-heterogeneous social contexts. In the Detroit interviews, references to being old and the discussion of old age among persons in age-heterogeneous social contexts were typically "quiescent" in tone, i.e. when asked questions about being old, there was a tendency among respondents to remain silent. If they answered, they did not generally elaborate the meaning of old age but they rather appeared to avoid the subject. A typical response was, "What do you want to talk about old people for—let's talk about young people." In general, it was obvious that these respondents were not enthusiastic about elaborating their views of old age.

Some aged persons in age-heterogeneous contexts are likely to be alienated from themselves as old people. They respond to questions about old age "at a distance." Their references to the aged use the terms "they" or "them." They do not as often refer to old people as "we." The comparative frequency of these alternative kinds of references may be one way to operationalize old age alienation among the elderly. In any delineated time period during an interview, the aged located in various kinds of social contexts could be measured for degree of self-alienation by some kind of systematic counting procedure focusing on self-references. This would provide evidence of whether or not certain social contexts are associated with self-alienation in old age.

The process of emerging self-alienation among old people in age-heterogeneous social contexts is contingent on at least four conditions: (1) the social definitions of others affect a person's delineation and knowledge of himself, (2) persons tend to avoid meaningfully devalued objects, (3) peer-isolated old people respond as individuals to others' social definitions of the aged, and (4) age-heterogeneous social contexts maximize the peer-isolation of the elderly. Given that there are publicly-devalued definitions of old age in the United States, the process of emergent self-alienation in age-heterogeneous contexts operates in a manner such that an old person in this kind of context encounters definitions of his old age fairly individualistically. Moreover, these encounters involve negative delineations of old age. In a process that is chronic and cumulative, an elderly man or woman comes to realize that the public definition of his or her person is negative. Since there are few immediate peers who can easily serve as a group with whom to share and diffuse this kind of experience, an aged person hardly has any criterion by which to judge himself other than a devalued one.

Because the object of public definitions is a negative self, so is the personal perception of this object a negative self. To an old person, what he perceives in himself is a devalued entity. Since persons tend to avoid, or are disinterested in, devalued objects or situations, it should not be surprising that the aged avoid themselves. The process of perception and avoidance of a negative self is enhanced to the extent that public devaluations are increasingly pronounced and the elderly are aware of this. The outcome of such an alienating process is a collection of aged persons who are age-aware and possess negative self-images. This, as Barron (1953) states, is characteristic of minority-like behavior.

Among the four conditions listed above as influencing the impact of public devaluations on the self, the social context of personal responses to public devaluations is crucial. The context of responses, depending upon whether it is age-concentrated or age-heterogeneous, influences the definitions of self that the elderly come to have. In age-heterogeneous contexts, the elderly encounter devalued self-definitions as individuals and they respond likewise. In contrast to this, age-concentrated contexts serve as a kind of buffer to public definitions. In those contexts, encounters with public definitions of old age are shared. Negative definitions are likely to be responded to in a manner different from the responses of relatively peer-isolated persons. It is much easier to scoff at public definitions when scoffing is reinforced by the similar actions of others who share a person's experiences. This scoffing is one visible indicator of the denial of negative self-images.

Impressions of the self-referral of persons in age-concentrated contexts in Detroit suggest that self-referral is not as readily avoided as in age-heterogeneous contexts. Old people in age-concentrated contexts were more willing to discuss old age and the problems of being old. These persons were not as likely to want to avoid the subject as their age-heterogeneous peers. When they did discuss old age, they were generally not as "edgy" as the latter. It was more evident in age-concentrated social contexts that the responses of the elderly about the elderly were more "dignified" than in age-heterogeneous contexts. For one thing, the frequency of weeping while discussing the elderly and their everyday lives was greater in the latter than in age-concentrated contexts, individual activity resources being equal. Responses in age-concentrated contexts were more often penetrated with statements on the "dignity" of being old. On the whole, these persons are likely to be more visibly proud of their age than their age-heterogeneous counterparts.

At this point, the question may be raised of whether or not

age-concentration per se leads to the transformation of minority group behavior, with its negative age-awareness, into group-consciousness and more positive self-images. Evidence (Fisher, 1962; Rose, 1965a; Trela, 1971) suggests that in addition to simple age-concentration, *active* efforts at building group-consciousness are more likely to be located in age-concentrated contexts than in age-heterogeneous ones.

An area of age-concentration is likely to be the location of active, formal efforts to aid old people in various ways. First of all, it is usually fairly widely known that large concentrations of aged persons reside in certain residences in urban areas. And second, any efforts to aid the elderly are most efficiently focused on places where the aged are known to reside in large numbers. Directing aid at places of age-concentration provides services for many persons with relatively little effort. Such efforts as informing the aged of their "rights," of services available to them, of their interests in a variety of local and national political issues, and at organizing them are often aimed at age-concentrated contexts. These kinds of relatively formal efforts at directly or indirectly influencing group-consciousness are likely to be concomitants of "visible" age-concentration.

The *informal* aspect of life in age-concentrated social contexts also influences the process of emergent group-consciousness. When a collection of persons becomes concentrated, it is likely that, given common characteristics and external devaluation, they will come to conceive of themselves as a *group* being devalued. Each person does not encounter the full impact of negative self-definitions alone. Rather, in a group of persons, a person responds to devaluation as part of a larger entity. It is the group of which he is a part that is perceived as being devalued. A group, or shared response to devaluation more easily prevents the personal internalization of negative self-images than an individual response. Encounters with devaluations that are shared lead to more positive outcomes than the individual encounters more likely to occur among age-heterogeneous, peer-isolated elderly persons. For one thing, the ability to "deal" itself is not as affected by shared encounters as it is by isolated ones.

As an outcome of this approach to and argument on the emergence of group-consciousness, the following hypotheses are proposed:

> *Negative self-images are more prevalent among old persons in age-heterogeneous social contexts than in age-concentrated contexts, individual resources being equal.*
>
> *Group-consciousness is more evident in age-concentrated social contexts than in age-heterogeneous ones.*

Changing Negative Self-Images

Since there is reason to believe that negative public attitudes toward the aged lead to the development of age-awareness among the elderly with subsequent negative self-conceptions, the problem of the desirability of this becomes an issue. As far as social policy is concerned, what are the strategies available by which to work toward the eventual elimination of minority group status among many old people with its negative effect on the morale of such persons?

From the approach to emergent group-consciousness outlined above and schematized in Figure 5, it is evident that there are two general strategies available for altering negative self-images among the aged. One would focus on the attitudes of others toward old people. This strategy would involve efforts to alter public information, beliefs, and sentiments about the aged. It would not deal with the aged themselves, but rather with the attitudes and behavior of the non-aged—primarily attitudes, assuming that these social psychological entities predispose and control persons' behaviors. This strategy will be referred to as *liberal.*

The second strategy focuses on the group of aged persons themselves. Rather than being primarily an attitudinal approach, it emphasizes the development of group-consciousness and group-interested action among old people, with primary emphasis on organizing group action. This approach assumes that the self-conceptions of old people are sensitive to their actions and respond to the betterment of their everyday lot. This strategy will be referred to as *radical.* It attempts to alter the structure of the relationship between the aged and others.

Both of these strategies are potential ideological dimensions of social movements. The liberal strategy is likely to be linked with persons who conceive of themselves as social reformers. These are individuals whose leadership is characterized by efforts primarily aimed at reforming or reconstituting the sources of a vairety of public images of the aged. Such liberal leadership works rather closely with the non-aged. As a matter of fact, liberal leadership and efforts would maintain very little in the way of active involvement with the aged themselves. On the whole, this leadership generally conceives of its work as an educational effort, considering its goal as one of "educating the public."

The success of the liberal strategy of altering negative self-images depends critically on its progress in changing the attitudes of the non-aged—or better, the public (since the public may include some aged persons who have the behavioral characteristics of active, working adults). The practical problems of such a strategy and movement are at least twofold. First, efforts at educating the public or changing public attitudes are rather nebulous affairs. The salient public and its location are vague. Moreover, it is not clear what kind of educational effort will be persuasive. A second kind of practical problem is that there is not any guarantee that if in fact public attitudes are altered, the living situations of the aged that have emerged partially as an outcome of negative public attitudes will be altered in any way. What could occur is the eventual public celebration of old age in the midst of structured inequities. This would become more a triumph for the public and liberal leadership than for the collection of the aged "rank-and-file."

A radical old age movement (which need not be general, but may be several movements each focusing only on specific local issues) has a leadership distinct from that of its liberal counterpart. The bulk of activity of radical leadership is not primarily spent with the "opposition." If anything, this kind of leadership tends to be actively hostile about what it may refer to as the "vacillation," "sham," and "lip-service" of the public and its representatives. It sees itself as clearly distinct from the non-aged (although leaders themselves may not be socially or chronologically old). It is easily exasperated by the complexities espoused by its opposition, considering these as oppositional attempts to mask "real" issues.

The success of a radical strategy of altering negative self-images and the lot of the elderly depends on resolving practical problems, again distinct from those of a liberal movement. First, since the aged were once young, a radical leadership has a natural disadvantage in maintaining the credibility of its legitimacy and the legitimacy of its strategy. For radical leadership, this is a problem that is likely to be perceived as one of overcoming a belief in "false" interests among the aged. Because of this problem, it would not be surprising that such leadership would devote its efforts to establishing the fact of old age in the minds of the elderly and dignifying some of its characteristics. Such efforts are likely to be verbally hostile to an opposition as well as consciously conspiratorial in its images of it. Aside from persuasion, a second practical problem for a radical leadership in an old age movement is organizational. The effort to establish legitimacy in ideology and leadership, and the conscious establishment of an opposition, indirectly would be an attack on organizational problems in that it would tend to unify the group itself. However, aside from this, major efforts at consolidating a collection of persons into an active bloc further coalesces them. Efforts may be directed at building a bloc of votes able to be focused on issues of importance to the aged as an interest group (cf. Palmore, 1969, p. 56). Consolidation may also be utilized to force change in local sources of deprivation in old age, such as collectively withholding the payment of rents in order to influence changes in some aspect of local living. The major practical problem of these kinds of efforts is consolidation and co-ordination.

Given the foregoing dimensions of liberal and radical strategies for changing negative self-images and/or everyday life in old age, it appears that, based on the approach to emergent group-consciousness taken here, each strategy has particular social conditions making it most likely to develop. If the elderly are age-concentrated in some manner (through either physical or communicative concentration), they are likely to become group-conscious and efforts are also likely to emerge to organize and thereby capitalize on this concentration. If the aged remain a simple collection of persons that more or less react individually (as a sub-public) to public devaluation, then they are likely to behave as a minority group rather than an interest group. Any strategy for change emerging with this more individualistic kind of social composition of elderly persons is likely to be intimately linked with the public and be reformist in character.

Although the approach to group-consciousness in old age taken here has focused on the interaction between collections or groups of old people, on the one hand, and external groups, on the other, there is a developmental aspect to emerging group-consciousness itself. It is likely that the career of emerging consciousness is such that its first stage is based on the aged as a minority group. The movements of this stage are likely to be liberal in character. Radical movements usually occur after the emergence of liberal attempts at change, the latter sometimes being transformed into and sometimes coming to exist alongside the former. Although there are these kinds of natural historical stages in the careers of many general social movements, what is being stated in addition to this here is that such stages are not simply "natural," but rather that the emergence of each is dependent on the internal and external social relations of a collection or group of people.

SOCIAL PERCEPTIONS OF OLD AGE

The foregoing approach to group-consciousness has located two important sources of influence on the development of self-awareness among the aged. One of these is external and is located in the public or social perceptions of the aged; the other is internal to groups of old people and results from the nature of social relationships within them. What is the evidence available on the social perceptions of old age?

To make an overall judgment on this evidence is somewhat problematic because it is both general and specific, i.e. some studies have tapped public attitudes toward and stereotypes of old people per se while other studies have measured public perceptions of specific aspects of being old. Perceptions of the aged have varied depending upon which of these two is considered. In a review of findings and research procedures used to measure attitudes toward old people, McTavish (1971, p. 97) implies that the negative stereotypes of old age and old people are general attitudes toward the aged. He suggests that the negativity of stereotypes is uneven and that general negativity may vary significantly from more positive perceptions of specific aspects of old age and the elderly. Referring to a list of selected items used in various investigations of acceptance or rejection of old people, McTavish (1971) states:

> . . . about a quarter of these respondents are willing to agree with those scale items which are somewhat more central to an over-all personal rejection or prejudice toward old people, although it could be argued that even some of these statements should be considered relatively remote indicators of the respondent's personal rejection of the elderly. Many scale items used in scales reflect attitudes about the prospect of aging or undesirable personal traits rather than attitudes toward the elderly themselves (p. 97).

Studies of the social perception of old people as a category, or old age generally, may be divided into two classes, depending upon whether they have examined perceptions cross-societally or within a single society among its individual members (McTavish, 1971). Although there is some contrary evidence, cross-societal studies indicate that attitudes toward the aged are most favorable in agrarian societies, becoming progressively negative with increasing industrialization and urbanization. Individual-level studies of perceptions of old age have generally been conducted within relatively modern societies. These studies, on the whole, tend to conclude with findings of highly negative stereotypes. As McTavish (1971) states:

> Stereotyped views of the elderly uncovered in various studies include views that old people are generally ill, tired, not sexually interested, mentally slower, forgetful and less able to learn new things, grouchy, withdrawn, feeling sorry for themselves, less likely to participate in activities (except, perhaps, religion), isolated, in the least happy or fortunate time of life, unproductive, and defensive in various combinations and with varying emphases (p. 97).

In another review of studies of social perceptions of generational differences, Bengtson (1971) summarizes various findings by stating:

> . . . this research seems to indicate: (1) that old people are viewed more negatively than other age groups; (2) that old people themselves tend to believe the negative stereotypes attributed to their age group; (3) that young people are positively valued, if not for their behavior at least for their potential (pp. 85-86).

Various pieces of research on attitudes toward the aged have appeared now for about two decades. The pioneering work in this area was launched by Tuckman and Lorge in 1952 and 1953. They developed two instruments which have been applied subsequently to a variety of persons for their perceptions of the aged. These persons ranged from college students to parents of college students, various levels of high school students, people differentially experienced with the aged, and different occupational and professional groups.

Both of the Tuckman-Lorge scales consisted of a list of stereotyped statements about old people's behavior, one of older workers and the other of old people in general. These statements were collected from various sources such as employers and persons who work with the elderly. Respondents were requested to show whether they agreed or disagreed with each of the statements listed by circling the "yes" or "no" answers provided. A respondent's score was a simple total of the number of "yes" answers circled.

The original Tuckman-Lorge scales have been revised by varying the instructions, reducing the number of items given, and changing the context of scale administration. In addition to these, several other separate instruments for measuring social perceptions of old age have emerged. These include scales of mixed negative and positive items of prejudice (Kogan, 1961), semantic differential scales for rating the perceptions of various age groups (Rosencranz and McNevin, 1969), and a modification of the Twenty Statements Test designed for eliciting open-ended responses from students about old people as a group (McTavish, 1971).

Correlates of Perceptions of Old Age

General social perceptions of old age have been found to be negative in industrial societies with a few exceptions. What have been the correlates of variations in these general negative perceptions? Are certain factors associated with a lessening of negativity in perception?

Insofar as there are variations in social perception that are fairly consistently associated with particular social character-istics, it could be concluded that the public perception of old age is somewhat uneven, i.e. not exclusively negative. Riley and Foner (1968) suggest this in their review of studies of popular stereotypes of old people. This kind of suggestion, however, is directed at and meant to be a criticism of the proposition that there is a universal negativity in the perception of old age. It does not deny that there is a widely prevalent negativity in this perception.

There is evidence that the public evaluation of the health of old people varies by age. Shanas (1962), in a national survey of 2500 adults over twenty-one, found that the public in general rates the health of older persons as "fair" in a choice between "good," "fair," or "poor." Comparing the general public (21+) with old people as a group, Shanas also found that the public underestimates the "good" state of health defined by the aged themselves.

Kogan and Wallach (1961) conducted a study of persons' evaluation of various stages of the life cycle ranging from infant and youth to middle age, elderly, old age, and death. Their sample consisted of 268 persons over forty-seven years old and students enrolled in psychology classes. Among both men and women and regardless of age, evaluations of the elderly, old age, and death stages were negative on the semantic differential. However, older persons were not as negative as the young about the later stages of life. This was true for both men and women. McTavish (1971) also found age differences in the perception of the aged within each sex category as well as when holding ethnic and marital status constant.

Social class and education may influence the negativity of

the perception of old age. The evidence on these correlates of perception is, however, somewhat uneven. Neugarten and Peterson (1957), in a study of 240 subjects aged forty to seventy, found that middle class respondents are more likely to perceive old age in terms of leisure and relaxation, while working class respondents were most likely to be concerned with the financial and health problems of old age. In contrast to this finding on social class and social perception, however, McTavish (1971) reports that in a 1965 national survey which he directed, little association was found between these two variables. At least two studies (Merrill and Gunter, 1969; Troll and Schlossberg, 1970) found that higher levels of education are associated with less negatively stereotyped conceptions of old age.

One final correlate of variations in perception of old age has been contact or interaction with the elderly. Of all the correlates of perception mentioned above, this is perhaps the most significant in relation to attempts at changing attitudes. The contact between varied age-groups has been the center of much age-oriented public debate and public policy making in recent years. The question of the extent and quality of contacts between age-groups has underpinned much of the discussion on housing and the issue of whether age-integration or age-segregation is most beneficial to old people.

Proshansky, and Chein (1954) define prejudice as,

> . . . an ethnic attitude in which the reaction tendencies are predominantly negative. In other words, for us a prejudice is simply an unfavorable ethnic attitude (p. 1022).

If the aged are considered to be a minority group, then attitudes toward the aged, insofar as they are negative, are analyzable in the same terms as are prejudiced attitudes in general. Given this similarity, what may be hypothesized about the relationship between contact and prejudice against the aged from what is known about contact and prejudice in general?

Before extrapolating from the general studies of the relationship between contact and prejudice, mention should be made of existing gerontological studies on the subject. As McTavish (1971) indicates, the available evidence has been somewhat contradictory. At least one study (Bekker and Taylor, 1966) found that in a multi-generational sample, students having had experiences with great-grandparents show evidence of less old age prejudice than those with grandparental experience only. The evidence that closeness of contact reduces prejudice toward old age is not corroborated in other studies however.

Perhaps the hypothesis of prejudice reduction with increasing inter-generational contact as conceived in gerontological studies is too simple. In discussing the general relationship between contact and prejudice, Allport (1958) concludes that there is sufficient evidence available that prejudice may not be reduced as a simple function of contact. Citing one study among others, he states:

> In an unpublished study of topical life histories (written on the subject, "My experiences with and attitudes toward minority groups") it was found that contact was frequently mentioned as a factor. But while the autobiographers reported that contact *lessened* their prejudice on 37 occasions, they also report that it *increased* their prejudice on 34 occasions. Obviously, the effect of contact will depend upon the kind of association that occurs, and upon the kinds of persons who are involved (p. 251).

Given that not only the extent of contact but its quality also influences prejudice, it is possible that the unevenness in gerontological data on contact and prejudice may have resulted from not attending to the nature of contacts. This alone might have confounded the relationship between frequency of contact and prejudice.

There is another dimension to studies of attitude change that is relevant to generating hypotheses on contact with and prejudice against the aged. This is the dimension of dissonance (cf. Festinger, 1957). Assuming that persons feel strained when experiencing the influence of contradictory or dissonant percepts, it follows that the greater the dissonance in perception the more effort a person will exert to avoid sources of dissonance. For example, in a study of a group of persons who predicted the end of the world, Festinger, Riecken, and Schachter (1956) found that those persons who were most committed to the group's belief system (group leaders) most successfully avoided the demoralizing effects of the world's not ending at a specific time and day when that time passed. Those persons less committed to the group and its beliefs were quite dismayed at the outcome of events, felt they could no longer adhere to the group's beliefs, and left the group. The relevance of the dimension of and evidence on dissonance to old age prejudice reduction is that, in addition to the impact of (1) frequency of inter-generational contact, and (2) the quality of such contact on prejudice against the aged, (3) constraining commitments to prejudiced attitudes may affect sensitivity to frequency and quality of contact. On the basis of the foregoing evidence, then, it is conceivable that commitments to old age prejudices may be so strong that any evidence (through contacts or purely informational) tending to contradict these negative predispositions may be perceived and then be forgotten, excepted, or avoided. Such commitment, for example, might be most typical among those persons who become leaders in "youth" movements or youth-oriented associations.

Although the foregoing three factors (commitment to prejudiced beliefs, frequency, and quality of contact) by no means exhaust the conditions affecting prejudice, they are nonetheless important influences on this kind of attitude. Because they have been found to affect prejudice in general, this may be extrapolated onto prejudice against the aged.

The simple proposition that frequency of inter-generational contact reduces prejudice against old people may be elaborated into at least the following two hypotheses:

> *Among non-aged persons with little or no commitment to age-prejudice, frequent contact with old people of a positive quality is associated with relatively low prejudice while frequent negative contact is associated with higher prejudice.*
>
> *Among non-aged persons with extensive commitments to age-prejudice, there is little or no relationship between frequency or quality of contact with old people and prejudice.*

These hypotheses suggest that frequency of contact per se should not be associated with any particular level of prejudice against the aged. If contacts are positive, for example, those persons with the most frequent contacts of this quality should have a lower negative predisposition toward the aged than those with fewer contacts. If the quality of contacts is negative, frequent contact should be associated with greater prejudice than either frequent or infrequent positive contact, as well as with infrequent negative contact.

INTRA-GROUP PATTERNS OF CONSCIOUSNESS

Thus far in this chapter, an approach to emerging group-consciousness in old age has been outlined with supporting evidence of the generally negative character of attitudes toward old people and old age. What evidence exists on how age-concentrated old people define themselves, i.e. what is the influence of social context on such definitions?

On the whole, the evidence that has been systematically collected on the extent of group-consciousness among old people in age-concentrated social contexts is rather limited. Two kinds of age-concentrated contexts have been examined: (1) age-concentrated residential contexts, and (2) age-homogeneous voluntary associations. Studies of both and the attitudinal correlates of being a member of either have shown that membership is associated with relatively high group and political consciousness.

These studies are limited in two ways. First, the fact is that only a few pieces of research available systematically focus on the effects of age-concentration among the aged on political consciousness (e.g. Rose, 1965a; Trela, 1971). Second, these studies are not longitudinal and thereby make it difficult to conclude that age-concentration in the form of residential concentration or age-homogeneous voluntary association causes group or political consciousness. The possibility that politically conscious old people may "naturally" seek membership in voluntary associations or differentially select themselves into age-concentrated residential contexts cannot be ruled out easily.

Before discussing the available evidence on the relationship between age-concentration and group-consciousness, mention should be made of a research design that could avoid the necessity of conducting longitudinal analyses and still enable one to conclude that age-concentration affects (rather than is associated with) group-consciousness, if data fall in the hypothesized direction. Such a design would initially involve drawing a sample of old people from age-concentrated and from age-heterogeneous social contexts. The sampling would stratify contexts so as to maximize variation in the independent variable, namely, age-concentration.

The difference between this particular design and others is that, in the process of sampling, evidence would have to be collected that made it clear that the recruitment of persons to social contexts was *independent* of group-consciousness. It would have to be shown that group-conscious old people do not over-select themselves to that kind of context which would support the hypothesis being tested.

Depending upon the process by which persons come to reside in social contexts, one or two types of evidence would have to be collected as proof of the absence of differential self-selection to particular ones. If, on the one hand, the process of recruitment to contexts is a "natural" one in which old people make a decision to move into them and subsequently do so, the evidence that is needed is of one type only, namely, that the group-consciousness of old people who are recruited is independent of the context into which a person moves. If, on the other hand, the process of recruitment to differential social contexts is a two-step affair involving the decision to move into one of them by an old person as well as a selection by officials of the contexts from among persons who have decided to move, evidence offered as proof of the absence of self-selection would have to be of two types. First, as in the "natural" process above, proof of random, context selection among aged movers would be necessary. Even if the "natural" process were fairly random, however, this does not guarantee that particularly group-conscious old people from among a fairly random sample of applicants would not be selected by officials of certain contexts. Because of this latter two-step kind of recruitment in some cases, a second kind of evidence of the absence of differential selection would be necessary to establish the initial independence of variables, namely, evidence of official recruitment on the basis of factors other than group-consciousness.

What kinds of evidence would constitute proof of the initial independence of study variables? If recruitment is a two-step process, two kinds of data would serve as proof. First, the official rules of recruitment stipulating minimal and maximal selection criteria would indicate the general nature of selection to contexts under any official's particular jurisdiction. These rules should indicate the basis upon which applicants are "officially" selected by officials. If there is no official sanctioning of any specific kind of recruitment on the basis of group-consciousness, this could serve as one kind of evidence of initial independence. Since all formal organizations have some kind of informal life, a second kind of data would extend the case for the initial independence of study variables. This kind of data could be generated through interviews with officials on the nature of the recruitment process. For example, officials might be asked: "Other than on the basis of official rules, what criteria do you use, if any, in selecting persons for the residences in your charge?" Or, "Are there particular kinds of persons that you tend either to recruit or to avoid in the selection process even if they do, like others, meet official requirements?" It is not the richness or dearth of answers that is of interest here. Rather, it is whether or not there are consistent or fairly frequent answers indicating recruitment on the basis of the dependent variable of the study.

In both simple and two-step recruitment, another kind of data would be necessary as proof of the absence of differential self-selection either to a particular context or to a list of applicants to a particular context. This data, on personal self-selection, could be collected by interviewing residents of, or applicants to, varied contexts about their reasons for deciding to move or apply to move into them. It would probably take at least two kinds of techniques to generate responses specifically centered on reasons that might deal with group-consciousness. First, some attempt would have to be made to reconstruct the time of moving in the mind of the respondent in order to psychologically set him to respond in terms of the events and his thoughts at that time of his life. Second, deliberate probing of reasons for moving other than officially sanctioned ones would increase the chances of group-conscious responses emerging.

Since there is available evidence that membership in voluntary associations is related to political and social awareness of various kinds (Berelson, Lazarsfeld & McPhee, 1954; Maccoby, 1958), a count of the number of such associational memberships prior to moving could serve as an indicator of possible group-consciousness. If persons with specific numbers or types of associational memberships (especially age-linked memberships) tend not to self-select to particular kinds of social contexts, this fact can serve as further evidence of the initial independence of study variables.

A "critical" design testing the hypothesis that age-concentration affects group-consciousness would sample social contexts in which there is an over-selection of group-conscious old people into age-heterogeneous social contexts rather than age-concentrated ones. If cases of such differential selection were found and age-concentrated social contexts still showed proof of greater group-consciousness on the average among their members than age-heterogeneous contexts, a strong argument supporting the hypothesis would have been made.

A "critical" design in studies focusing on two-step recruitment contexts would sample contexts in which official recruitment to age-concentrated contexts tends to deny admission to group-conscious old people. The conservative nature of official recruitment makes it likely that such a "critical" design may unwittingly be the outcome of any study testing a hypothesis on age-concentration and group-consciousness, in any case.

Studies of Age-concentration and Consciousness

The following studies of membership in age-homogeneous voluntary associations and its effect on group-consciousness are problematic in the sense that they do not establish a basis for making causal statements on the relationship between variables. It is not clear in these studies whether associational membership makes for attitudinal changes or whether existing group-consciousness among some old people influences the likelihood that they will seek age-homogeneous association.

Rose (1965a) conducted a study of group-consciousness among the elderly. His primary concern in this research was whether or not those persons who could be characterized as group-conscious differed significantly in behavior and attitudes from those aged persons who are not group-conscious. His working definition of group-consciousness was the criterion of membership in formal voluntary associations exclusively for the aged. Persons in such associations were assumed to be group-conscious. A sample was drawn so as to facilitate comparisons of behavior and attitudes between group-conscious and non-group-conscious old people. Three kinds of organizations were selected for the group-conscious stratum of the sample: age-oriented recreational associations organized by the non-elderly, an action-oriented "Old-Timers' Club," and a politically-oriented organization of old people. The non-group-conscious stratum of the sample was drawn from a house-to-house survey of the aged in the Minneapolis area.

The findings show that regardless of associational membership, there is little reason to believe that the aged in general are isolated and disengaged. Among those persons who are not members of voluntary associations, the primary reason given for their non-membership (when they had held membership earlier in life) is that they were forced out rather than having voluntarily withdrawn.

Membership in age-homogeneous voluntary associations is associated with greater life satisfaction than non-membership. Persons with memberships are more likely than non-members to state that they associate more with their own age-group, as they grow older.

The significant finding on the correlates of age-concentration in social contexts is that among the aged with age-homogeneous membership in contrast to non-members, daily concerns are more extensively centered on the problems of old people. Members more frequently converse about health and other problems of old age. Their conversations are more age-conscious than that of non-members. It is apparent, in Rose's data, that members of age-homogeneous voluntary associations are more greatly conscious of their interests as a group distinct from other age-groups. For example (Rose, 1965a, p. 35), members are more likely to say that there should be more organizations for the elderly, that the elderly "ought to organize to demand their rights," and that "older people ought to be more active in politics." Moreover, aged members show evidence that group-consciousness is not associated with a negative reaction to external devaluation of old age but rather associated with a positive evaluation of age. A higher proportion of members say that they are "proud to have reached [their] present age."

The foregoing data on the positive self-identity associated with age-concentration supports the approach to emergent group-consciousness outlined earlier in this chapter. Rose's data suggest, as was mentioned earlier, that self-devaluation is an outcome of peer-isolated encounters with and responses to negative attitudes toward old age. The data support our earlier suggestion that positive self-reactions to negative attitudes toward the aged are associated with age-concentration—in this case, age-homogeneous associational membership.

More recently, Trela (1971) conducted a study of the political consequences of old age associational membership. This was similar in design to Rose's (1965a) earlier research. The major focus of Trela's study was on the question of whether or not "senior centers" (as age-homogeneous voluntary associations),

> ... provide a context for heightened sociopolitical consciousness and activity, and whether members of such associations, compared to those who have no group membership or are members of mixed generational groups only, share expectations that favorably orient them toward political activity governed by their common age status p. 118).

Trela's sample was drawn from a listing of elderly persons contacted as part of a recruitment drive for a local senior center in Cleveland. The sample was stratified between those who joined and became members and those who did not as an outcome of the drive.

Political consequences of membership were tapped by asking persons with varying degrees of participation to indicate, on a checklist, whether or not they had discussed a variety of topics while attending the center. Examples of listed topics were "argued about politics," "discussed politics," "talked about problems of old people," and "talked about riots and demonstrations." Trela found that the more often subjects attended the senior center, the more likely they said that they had discussed the above topics.

The political behavior and orientation of senior center members and members of other old age groups were compared with that of elderly persons sampled with no associational memberships or memberships in mixed generational groups. Members of the senior center and other old age groups were most likely to have engaged in varied political activities in the preceding three months. They were also the persons most predisposed toward joining a political organization of elderly persons. Persons with mixed generational group memberships were the least predisposed toward joining such an organization.

Much of the foregoing discussion of the degree of political consciousness associated with age-concentration and age-exclusiveness is founded on the proposition that the "objective" distribution and density of persons, under concentrated conditions, are more likely to become transformed into subjectively meaningful group behavior than under less concentrated conditions. Since some of the evidence for this is less than definitive, attempts could be made to make future studies more so. Fisher (1962) summarizes the issue as follows:

> We have no way of knowing at present whether old-age movements would score high on such a measure of segregation. It is one plausible explanation of the disciplined political behavior of such groups. It is not, however, the participation in pension movements which produces the segregation although this is doubtless a reenforcing factor. It is far more probable that it has been the segregation of the aged which brings about the development and strength of the old-age movements (p. 44).

MECHANISMS FOR SPREADING CONSCIOUSNESS

With increasing age-concentration (either residential or associational), it is likely that what was previously only age-awareness becomes group-consciousness. It has been hypothesized above that not only is group-consciousness a later stage in the career of an emergent interest group, but that this later stage is significantly dependent on the concentration of elderly persons. Given relatively dense age-concentration, typical of type I social contexts (see Fig. 2, Chap. III), it should be the case that group-consciousness is comparatively high among residents. There should be fairly well-defined processes or mechanisms by which group-consciousness emerges or is sustained within a collection of age-concentrated persons. What kinds of processes influence group-consciousness and the sympathetic awareness of mutual interests?

These processes may be categorized into two classes. One has a source *outside* collections of age-concentrated elderly persons. Processes with external sources typically emerge out of the actions of a variety of persons from outside age-concentrated contexts who direct two kinds of efforts toward the contexts: attempts at (1) directly organizing persons in some group-interested effort such as voting or petitioning (cf. Pinner *et al.*, 1959; Rose, 1962b), and (2) indirectly influencing group-consciousness through a variety of educational efforts specifically of interest to the aged such as "health talks," income maintenance and social security classes, or planned discussions on community events for old people. Both of these are more likely to be found operating among the aged in age-concentrated residential and associational contexts than in age-heterogeneous ones for at least two reasons. First, high concentrations of old people are more visible than the aged in age-heterogeneous social contexts. This makes it likely that there is available public information on the location of such contexts for persons or agencies interested in directing their efforts toward them. Second, even if public information on the location of all elderly persons were available, the costs of efforts aimed at age-concentrated old people are much less than those efforts directed toward relatively dispersed persons.

A second class of mechanisms for spreading consciousness has its source *within* collections of elderly persons. These are social processes which generate solidarity among persons in age-concentrated contexts as a function of the facts that the chance of encounters occurring between them is high and that similar kinds of persons are readily available to each other as sources of social interaction. These mechanisms are of two kinds: (1) formal group events planned by aged residents for themselves that are specifically directed at promoting solidarity such as residence councils, and (2) informal group gatherings that tend to emerge as a result of common interest in some event, such as meeting to watch an age-oriented news program on television or meeting to watch or listen to some form of entertainment which is age-specific and commonly enjoyed.

In that aspect of the Detroit Study which focused on age-concentrated social contexts, it was obvious how the preceding informal processes operated to enhance a common consciousness among residents. In several instances while interviewing a subject, another resident of the building would knock on the door of the interviewee and either inform or remind him that there was a television program to be shown that evening on some topic of interest to the elderly. In one case, a respondent had been perusing the evening's programming before the interviewer approached her. Upon entering her apartment, the interviewer noted that the respondent was reminding herself that she would have to tell her "lady-friends" down the hall about a particular "show" on nursing homes. That same evening, the small group of friends gathered to watch the program, discussing and agreeing or disagreeing over its contents. In this particular group, it was clear that the program had either spawned or enhanced a common negative sentiment against the homes. The next day, each of the members of the group who had gathered to watch the program were asked what they thought about "last night's TV show on nursing homes." Besides their own thoughts, each reinforced her opinion by adding that all of her friends felt the same about what they saw and heard. Two of the "watchers" even told the interviewer to ask a specific other "watcher" if the interviewer wanted to know how they felt.

The evidence for the group-consciousness effects of informal gatherings in age-concentrated contexts in Detroit was not collected completely from the recall of respondents. In several instances, interviews with subjects were conducted both before and after a gathering. This enabled a kind of quasi-experimental comparison to be made of its consciousness effects. Subjects who had not gathered to watch a program were also interviewed both before and after as a kind of control.

SUMMARY

In this chapter, we have outlined an approach to group-consciousness in old age. This approach focuses on the relationship between public evaluations of old age and the aged themselves. The nature of the reactions of old people to public devaluation appears to be influenced by their social contexts. On the basis of the approach taken as well as available evidence, two hypotheses were proposed on the reactions of old people to public devaluation in age-concentrated as opposed to age-heterogeneous social contexts.

Some of the existing evidence on public evaluations of the elderly was examined. On the whole, although there have been some exceptions, general evaluations have tended to be negative. It has been suggested that the negativity of evaluations varies with such factors as age, education, and contacts with the elderly.

Finally, the effect of age-concentration on a variety of political attitudes of old people was discussed. The few studies that deal with this have shown that there is a higher degree of political consciousness among the aged who are located in age-concentrated as opposed to age-heterogeneous associational contexts.

Chapter VII

THE MYTH OF
THE GOLDEN YEARS

A SPECIFIC APPROACH to the sociology of "normal" aging has been taken in the foregoing chapters. Because the commitment to an approach is, at bottom, not calculated but rather "chosen" on the basis of one's sentiments, once an approach has been taken, whether wittingly or not, a theorist has sided with one of a variety of choices and has made a value decision. Here, a "choice" has been made to assume the postulates of socio-environmentalism as opposed, for example, to the postulates of the popular notion of the golden years.

Not only is the matter of "choosing" an approach basically a value decision, but it may also be ideological. Certain postulates are more likely than others to lead to conservative support of ongoing social processes and events, while others are more likely to underpin liberal or radical sentiments toward these same processes and events.

Because all social theories have a basis in values and are potentially ideological, they are thereby also critical. Every approach to the social behavior of the aged, then, is to some degree a criticism of other approaches. Approaches vary in the extent that they are actively "critical" theories. This variation in the activeness of criticism is closely linked with whether assumptions chosen are conservative or not.

If assumptions or basic postulates are conservative, they underpin the defense of the social conditions of old age that exist. In this instance, there is little utility in criticism of other competing postulates and approaches since the conservative assumptions, in effect, are having "their way." The holders of conservative assumptions in approaches to old age are more likely to be apologetic than openly critical (although certainly apologetics may be interpreted as conservative criticism). They are also likely to celebrate the alignment of their approach with the "best of all possible worlds," and in extreme cases "the only viable world." They are not as likely to be as intellectually antagonistic as are holders of less conservative "critical" assumptions.

Non-conservative assumptions underlying approaches to the social life of old people lead to more actively critical intellectual styles. It is not unusual for critical approaches to be engaged in polemics against conservatives for a large share of their professional activities. They are more likely than the conservatives to be actively engaged in unmasking the myths of old age. They are also more likely to scoff at popular stereotypes of the golden years.

Given that any approach to old age is a potential source of criticism of other views of the same period of the life cycle, what dissensions about popular ideas of old age follow from the socio-environmental point of view? Let us focus on the golden years myth since it is a collection of popular conceptions about the elderly and their social behavior.

THE GOLDEN YEARS MYTH

Before outlining a criticism of the golden years myth from a socio-environmental point of view, a sketch of its major dimensions would be useful. How, then, do holders of the golden years idea portray (1) the social environment of the golden years, (2) the social interaction and activity of old people, (3) the health and income of the aged, and (4) their life satisfaction?

The golden years myth is a popular, conservative, often contradictory set of ideas about several aspects of the social life of old people. Although parts of it have affinities with either disengagement or activity theory, it still has a public, non-professional life of its own. It exists in several places such as popular magazines, retirement brochures, newspapers, and in other news and entertainment media as "human interest information" about the later years of life. It is not unusual to find an article on the golden years in the Sunday supplement section of American newspapers. What is characteristic of such public information on the golden years is that it is often glib, complacent, and on the whole celebrates old age as a generally peaceful, "kind," and happily "free-of-troubles" period of living. The portrait of elderly persons tends to be one of a collection of "nice, kind old ladies" that are "just wonderful people."

These images of the golden years contrast rather sharply with what is known about personal attitudes toward the aged through a variety of surveys. The contrast resounds of the statement: "They're happy and nice people, but I wouldn't want to live with them." The golden years myth represents a kind of guiltless complacency in the public. On the one hand, there is a general tendency to devalue the aged and avoid anything behaviorally "old," while on the other, there is a convenient general portrayal that all is well in old age. The myth allows the devaluation of old age to occur without remorse.

Social Environment Images

The social context of old age as portrayed by the myth is comprised of three types of images. One of these is that of the alleged general well-being of old people who continue to maintain their own neighborhood household. A second is that of the "retirement years" of persons who reside in a retirement community. And, a third is the image of the "convalescent home." These three images of felicitous social contexts correspond with some of the dimensions of types IV, III, and I social contexts, respectively (see Fig. 2, Chap. III). In some ways, the images differ radically from the dimensions of these types.

The first of these images, perhaps best captured by the phrase "grandmother's house," conceives of a self-sufficient couple in an older neighborhood of homes, who maintain a mutually satisfactory round of daily life. Both are portrayed as actively involved in a variety of crafts and hobby-like activities. Both maintain active local connections in neighborhoods that are "just as I remember them." Their social contexts are, however, sometimes hampered by rising crime rates, neighborhood transition, or declining social services. These last three, rather prevalent conditions, tarnish the golden years image of "grandmother's house."

On the whole, the public portrayal of an elderly person's household that characterizes old age as the golden years does not show evidence of concern with several kinds of urban residential environments. For example, the golden years image of the social environment does not extend to boarding homes, mixed-age apartment dwellings, or tenements. Rather, the urban household portrayed tends to be the single family home located in a neighborhood of similar homes. These homes are described as "neat, well-kept, and immaculate." Neighborhoods are pleasant, peaceful places.

The public image of "grandmother's house" may take on a sort of nostalgia in references to the "old neighborhood." There is a romantic kind of reminiscing associated with this that consists in a series of exchanges between middle-adult persons reminding each other of various dimensions of daily life in the old neighborhood. There are two phrases common to such reminiscing, one or the other being used depending upon whether the nostalgia is recollective or comparative. When it involves a series of recollective exchanges, it is often penetrated with, "You remember . . ." or "Remember when. . . ." When it is comparative, it tends to be exemplary. Examples of life in this or that old neighborhood are cited as contrasts to the so-called "rat-race" in the suburbs. In these comparative exchanges, there are often vague references to "there" followed by a description of how persons in such environments enjoy their neighborhood and how intimate and "helpful" are the relationships between persons.

One very common image of the social context of elderly people is that of the old style ethnic neighborhood. A mental picture emerges of well-kept houses with a variety of local services within walking distance. Thoughts occur of "mama and papa" going to *shul*. Daily visits to the baker and the meatman come to mind. This is not entirely recollective, for if "mama" is still in the old neighborhood, she tends to be linked with these kinds of images, images of people with strong ties to their locales and intense pride in property.

This golden portrayal of "grandmother's house" is not without contradiction. It is often confounded with the knowledge of change, for example, changing neighborhood composition and the flight of local services to more lucrative, stable, and less precarious markets. The two sides of this contradictory image of the golden years neighborhood tend to emerge in different circumstances. The felicitous side is most visible in popular publications and nostalgic exchanges. The more negative side becomes vivid when visiting or thinking about visiting the aged in their households. The negative side has a way of being forgotten when not in the neighborhoods. The golden years idea is a very enticing one.

A second golden image of old age social contexts is that of the retirement community. This image is prevalent in two places: in the thoughts of persons about their retirement and more visibly in the advertisements and popular portrayals of such communities (cf. Gersuny, 1970).

If any one thing is outstanding in the image of the retirement community, it is that of references to climate. Although many of these communities indeed are located in areas of the country such as Florida, California, and Arizona which have warm climates, the image of climate tends to be epitomized as one of blissful sunshine. The sun becomes part of a variety of epithets such as "the sunshine years" or names given to these communities such as "Sunset Village." It should be noted that there is not only a tendency to utilize various kinds of climatological terms in the image of retirement communities, but that these terms often refer to the climax of states of the climate—hardly ever the initial states. For example, "sun" is often coupled with "set," rarely with "rise."

The golden image of retirement communities is advertised as a form of escape. It is portrayed as a holiday, in fact, a perpetual vacation. It is a geographical resolution of all the problems of being old. By some miraculous means, locating oneself in such communities marks the beginning of an entirely new life. The ads containing this image are quite alluring. They try to entice elderly persons to them.

The social context portrayed in retirement community images often has the physical appearance of a resort motel. It is shown in a variety of glossy color photos as grassy, flower-ridden, sunny, well-kept, and convivial. It is not unusual to find scenes of gathered persons in amicable poses. These all tend to be portraits of fun and enjoyment.

There is a third image of golden social contexts. This is the image of the convalescent home. More than the two foregoing images of social contexts, extensive euphemistic efforts are involved in the advertisements portraying these facilities. Since these in fact often are terminal environments for old people, the necessity of attracting clientele in order to remain solvent places pressure on the owners of these homes to avoid as much as possible their terminal character as well as the behavior of some terminal occupants.

One highly euphemistic effort is the naming of the facilities. Owners confront the well-known repugnance of the aged toward "nursing" homes. It is not surprising to find that many of the facilities are labeled convalescent or geriatric centers. Some are simply labeled, for example, the "Rosewood Home" [fictitious].

In the various pamphlets and announcements distributed by these facilities, it is common to find a portrayal of an environment that is said to "take care of all the needs" of the elderly. The atmosphere of such homes is described as "warm, tender, and concerned." Rather than being an ode to the sun, the image portrayed is one of "tender, loving care."

On the whole, the golden image of social environments for old people is one of "life without any problems." The images of all social contexts portray the necessary coping ability of the aged as minimal. In short, these images describe social environments as placing few demands on their everyday lives, thereby posing little or no burden to them.

Images of Social Interaction and Activity

The golden years myth also contains specific images of social interaction and activity among old people. Not only are social contexts considered felicitous but so are the relationships between old people as well as their activity. Four images of interaction and activity should be noted: (1) the idea of growing old together, (2) the indulgent intergenerational portrayal of the aged, (3) the ideal active "busyness" of the elderly and (4) the simple advice of planning for retirement.

The image of growing old together is a popular one in the golden years myth. It conceives of old age as a period of the life cycle in which a married couple now has time to "enjoy each other and each other's company." It is a time for indulging in a renewed mutual interest without the problems of childcare and work. All of this is centered on the elderly *couple* and their alleged "shared, enriching growth" together.

There is a deviant side to the image of growing old together. This is the side of the widow and widower, especially the widower. The golden years myth does not usually carry an image of a spouseless elderly male. This smacks of isolation, inactivity, household dishevelment, and brooding. If anything, the image is much more sympathetic to the spouseless elderly female, for it is difficult publicly to portray an indulgent, tender, child-oriented old man. The mental associations of the term "old lady" tend to be thought of as more benign than those of "old man."

The daily life of the elderly couple is epitomized by images of active involvement in affairs that tend to have a quasi-rural character. They are portrayed as concerned with a variety of household activities such as making their own foodstuffs and "being handy." All of this occurs in an unhurried, idyllic everyday life style.

The social world of the elderly couple extends to a fair amount of involvement in church-related activities. It also extends to interest, as a couple, in different kinds of community-oriented affairs. A great deal of this is volunteer work. All in all, the image is one of a self-sufficient elderly man and his wife.

Another image of the social interaction of the elderly is the portrayal of intergenerational indulgence. The image denotes the most significant social relationship of the elderly couple as being with their children and grandchildren. Presumably, this is expressed through a kind of selflessness in the couple, an oblivious interest in self in the presence of children and grandchildren. It is a child-oriented altruism. From the point of view of their children, the elderly couple is considered a source of refuge for any conceivable problem. The couple is portrayed as "living for their children."

Not only is this image of elderly altruism described in various popular publications, media, and pamphlets, but there is an attitudinal counterpart to this also. The image emerges in discussions with the aged themselves. For example, in the Detroit Study, it was not rare to hear references to children and grandchildren in various stages of interviewing. These references not only occurred in direct probes of what kinds of social involvements respondents felt that older persons should pursue, but they were mentioned also whenever respondents thought of those activities they wished they could pursue. Respondents typically would make references to what their children expected of them when they were discussing their relationships with them. A common statement was, "My daughter comes to me whenever she needs something and she knows I'll help her." This was often associated with references to the happiness that such availability brought to the lives of the elderly. As some would say, "This is what parents are for, isn't it?

If these foregoing kinds of attitudinal data on intergenerational social interaction were translated into life satisfaction, there would be a question of whether or not they were images. However, the reason why they are referred to as attitudinal aspects of popular images of altruism is that the same respondents who express altruistic sentiments toward their children and grandchildren say that their children and grandchildren "make them nervous." A typical statement is: "I don't mind seeing them frequently and wish I could, but I wouldn't like to live with them." This expression is not made in response to their children's wishes for independent living. Rather, it expresses old people's realistic feelings that their own needs, interests, and life style as elderly persons are in many ways different from those of their children. Everyday life for older persons must be sustained on its own terms.

The child-orientation of the elderly, then, has two sides. One appears to be an expression of an altruistic involvement with their children. The other side expresses the somewhat negative reactions associated with too extensive intergenerational interaction. The first of these is a personal expression of adherence to a public image of altruism.

There is a third image of social interaction and activity. It portrays the elderly as "busy." They are described as having highly involved daily lives, although their activities appear to be trivial. Not only are they considered highly involved, but the popular descriptions of this are rather patronizing. It is not uncommon to find references to the active and involved life of the golden years that have a tone of sympathetic amusement. Occasionally, one has the distinct feeling that children are being discussed in references to the aged and their activity.

The image of being "busy" avoids an important aspect of the life of some old people, namely, social isolation and depression. These are not part of the golden years myth. If these are mentioned at all, they are said to be negative consequences of an uninvolved life. The golden image of old age portrays activity and general "busyness" as the sources of life satisfaction. This "busyness" does not refer typically to intense social relationships, but rather to craft and hobby-life activities. It is not unusual to hear such panaceas as "get involved," or "keep busy" popularly expressed as solutions to the problem of life satisfaction in old age.

The logic of life satisfaction portrayed by the golden image of activity is simple. First, social integration is defined in stereotyped active, middle-adult terms. Being active means that one is not idle, that one works at some task or tasks, that one feels satisfaction with work, and that work occupies the bulk of a person's everyday life. Second, life satisfaction is said to be the fruit of work well done and done with zeal. Third, since gainful work of the kind typical of working adults is not generally available to elderly persons, then quasi-work is substituted. This quasi-work is "keeping busy." And fourth, it follows that the more one exerts active efforts at "keeping busy," the greater the life satisfaction.

On the face of it, this activity solution to life satisfaction in old age appears quite simple. It only involves the choice of becoming "busy" by an aged person. There is, however, one very critical assumption underlying this image of activity and life satisfaction in old age. There is also a hidden limitation in what is defined as social interaction by the golden image.

The assumption underlying the image of simply choosing to become involved in a variety of activities is that a person has the ability to actively carry out his choice. The assumption is that a choice is automatically translatable into activity. It is because of this assumption that the golden years solution to life satisfaction appears so simple. Occasionally, the assumption of active ability is quite evident in popular portrayals of the solution. For example, it is evident in such clichés as "Life is what you make it," and "You're as young as you feel."

Because the social integration of the elderly is portrayed as a function of a personal choice and the personal translation of this choice into active "busyness," non-integration and consequent life dissatisfaction also are considered matters of personal decision. If old people choose to remain inactive and become demoralized, then, as is popularly said, "You only have yourself to blame!" What emerges from this assumption on personal choice and personal ability is that an aged person is portrayed as solely responsible for whatever life style and state of mind he develops.

In addition to the assumption on personal ability underlying the golden image of activity, the definition of social integration is severely lmited. Assuming that all old people have the ability and that life satisfaction is a matter of choosing to be active, the image implies that it is only a particular kind of activity that leads to social integration, namely, involvement in the active world of quasi-work. The problem with this, however, is that there is a variety of everyday worlds in which to become involved in old age, not all of which are active, work-like worlds. In the non-active kinds of everyday world available to old people, social integration is not a function of "busyness." Rather, it may be an outcome of "idleness."

There is an image of social integration that does portray an "idleness" of sorts as embodying a source of life satisfaction. This is the golden image of everyday life in retirement communities. Popular literature dealing with life in these communities does not focus on inactivity, but generally shows daily life to be filled with a host of leisure activities. This is idleness of a special kind—an "idleness" that is work-like. Old people in retirement communities are portrayed as being intensely involved in recreational concerns. They are shown as working hard at play.

References to non-gainful activity in brochures and pamphlets on retirement communities are made in such a way that one may unwittingly read them as references to active involvement in "work." This occurs in an amusing and subtle linguistic turn of events. For example, the same words and phrases used to describe the working day of middle-adults are initially applied to the recreational activities of old people in these communities. At first, this is done with a usually clear reference to recreational and hobby-like activities as being the "work" or "active involvement" of the elderly. However, once this initial proviso has been made, further references to the activities of the aged in the communities are to "work" only. It is no longer in hobbies and games that older persons are described as being engaged. Rather, now, they are said to have "a busy day" or in the evening "to relax from the many things accomplished that day." The daily world of recreational activity is described in the same way as the world of work.

What is being sold in popular literature on the golden retirement years is nostalgia. It recalls the alleged fullness of daily life before retirement in which the activeness of physical or mental work led to a satisfying sort of exhaustion that "justified" a few hours of evening leisure. The image of the retirement community attempts to sell a romantic reconstruction of an earlier stage of the life cycle. Sheer rest is not being portrayed but rather a "full life for senior citizens."

There is a voluntaristic side to the image of everyday life in retirement communities that is analogous to the assumption on activity ability and social integration mentioned above. The "active fulfillment" of retirement communities is portrayed as "available to all." The only restriction is that one must have reached retirement age. Once this has occurred, the image may be realized by simply deciding to "make a change in your life."

For a man or woman approaching retirement, the preceding aspects of the image of the golden retirement years may lead to the internalization of expectations with similar contents. At a certain stage in their work lives, persons begin actively and conscientiously to think about retirement. It is not unlikely that their expectations of what life will be like at that time is influenced by popular images of it. These images of the golden years myth may become part of the plan that a person has for his post-retirement life. Insofar as the images that influence planning are simplistic and unreliable descriptions of retirement living, all the plans made by persons based on them may have rather demoralizing consequences upon retirement.

Although the golden image of retirement may not be a false portrayal of that stage of life for some persons, its internalization and extensive planning based upon it do not necessarily lead to life satisfaction for all. The image, its internalization, and extensive planning for some individuals may be a grand design of wishful thinking. The point is that neither the image, its internalization, nor planning alone or together necessarily leads to a golden retirement. The rationale for this will be discussed below in the section of this chapter which criticizes the golden years myth.

Images of Solvency

The popular portrayal of the golden years extends beyond general images of the world of retirement and its everyday activities. It is specific on a certain number of issues of old age, these being images of solvency and health.

The portrayal of solvency in old age, as with other aspects of the golden years myth, is a description of felicity. The problems of finances are said to be special in old age. They are special in the sense that they are a function of altered needs.

It is from the definition of these needs that the image of adequate income emerges. The elderly person, because of reductions in his needs, is said to have an adequate income from Social Security and other federal, state, and city old age benefits. "Adequacy" then easily leads to the conclusion that old age income is not a major problem for the aged.

This image of solvency is centered on an implicit argument that deals with the concept of human needs. All persons, regardless of age, are said to have a variety of needs that must be fulfilled in order to sustain life. These include various kinds of physiological sustenance and shelter. It may extend to the need for facilities such as education, job training, and transportation. In the argument, needs are put into a life span perspective. They are characterized as reaching a peak in early adult life, remaining fairly even throughout middle age, and declining upon reaching old age. In old age, persons are said to have fewer of these important needs than younger persons. The argument begins by citing particular kinds of needs and conceives of these as quantitatively declining with age.

Because persons have needs, conditions adequate to their fulfillment must exist if they are to lead satisfactory lives. Since needs are said to decline with age, the conditions necessary for their fulfillment also decline with age. The conditions required to sustain an older person, then, are said to be adequate at a lower level than that which is sufficient for a younger person.

This implicit argument underlying the golden image of income adequacy in old age rests entirely on the portrayal of a decline in particular needs common to middle-adults. What it avoids are the specific changes in needs that follow retirement and growing physically older. It ignores the likelihood that a new set of needs emerges, such as medication, special transportation, and companionship. When age-specific needs are ignored, it is not difficult to state that adequacy levels change with age. The problem, here, is that the everyday needs of the aged are defined in terms of the needs of younger persons and simply extrapolated onto old people.

The image of solvency that follows from this argument sustains the belief that the income maintenance programs that

currently exist are adequate for older persons. It is not un-
common to hear references to the periodic increases in Social
Security as attuned to rising prices. The image portrays those
monies provided to the aged through Social Security as adequate.
Moreover, it is said, those benefits are constantly increasing.
Besides this, the image is quick to add that the indirect income
provided through Medicare certainly makes the benefits of
Social Security sufficient.

There is also a "last straw" justification in the golden image
of diminished needs and adequate income among the aged. If
the noting of Social Security benefits and Medicare is not con-
vincing, reference is made to the provisions contained in Old
Age Assistance programs and Medicaid. As a matter of fact,
the literature of these programs itself is self-congratulatory for
its alleged comprehensiveness in maintaining income adequacy
for old people. It benevolently informs its aged clientele that
their needs are "covered" in a variety of circumstances from
short-term to chronic. If it isn't Social Security, it will be Old
Age Assistance. If it isn't Medicare, it will be Medicaid. One
finds a general "cradle-to-the-grave" gratuity in this portrayal.

Images of Health

The portrayal of health in old age from the point of view of
the golden years myth also "accentuates the positive." The
health image, however, is narrower than that of solvency. References to health are not typically made to a general state of good
health among old people in the same way that references to
Social Security are said to benefit "all" the aged. Perhaps the
only time in recent years that an image of the general good
health of the aged was publicly portrayed was at the initiation
of the Medicare and Medicaid programs. One heard of a forth-
coming "new era" in the health care of elderly people. The
programs were alleged to be a solution to the major problem
of growing old in America, namely, chronic illness and the high
cost of medical care. The generality of this health reference has
been the closest approximation to the generality of references to
income maintenance through the Social Security program.

The golden image of good health in old age has been typically more specific in its references than has the image of solvency. These more specific references are not as self-congratulatory as the latter, but they certainly tend to be more patronizing. Specific portrayals occur in two kinds of popular practices: (1) the exemplification of the "spry" and (2) the exaltation of extreme old age. These practices involve particular elderly persons who either exhibit some unusual degree of agility or who have lived into fairly old age.

Exemplifying the spry usually takes place in a rather theatrical setting. The practice popularly proceeds as follows. An aged man or woman is called upon to perform some act of sorts. Now, if it were not known who the performer was, usually the act would not be judged as either a feat or an exercise in mastery. However, what makes for audience applause and amazement is the knowledge that the performer is, in fact, an elderly person. Allegedly unusual agility or expertise is then congratulated as an example of a rare spryness. Finally, as the performer bows away from the stage, comments are made that have the combined tone of moralizing and glib wishes, expressing the desire of middle-adults in the audience "to be the same when we're that age."

The relationship between audience and spry performer is one that is usually highly patronizing. The relationship is similar to the indulgence of parents as they watch their children perform what, from nonparental eyes, might appear to be inane stunts: an old person performs, he is congratulated, and then dismissed.

What makes the portrayal of spryness golden is that such performances, for the audience, are examples of the maintenance of youth and establish the "fact" that being elderly need not lead to being feeble. This person is said to have "made the most of old age." He stands as an example of "what the later years can be." Again, the voluntaristic aspect of the golden years myth is evident. This performer is "living proof" of this.

Another kind of popular practice that specifies particular persons as portraits in golden health is the exaltation of extreme old age. Like the exemplification of spryness, this too has its routine practice. It also is a patronizing, amused, and momentarily awestruck relationship between audience and performer.

In this case, however, the performance usually takes the form of an interview rather than an act.

Before the interview begins, a man or woman of extreme old age is located. This kind of performance is not played by persons of age sixty or seventy. This is too young to exalt and certainly, because it is relatively common, would provide little or no "human interest" value. Rather, persons who are in their late eighties and preferably in their nineties approaching one hundred are typical interviewees.

The interview format is a popular one and proceeds through well-known stages. First, the respondent is asked to state his or her age. At this point, there are usually a few congratulatory comments and sighs made expressing admiration of having lived for so long. Second, the respondent may be asked his personal recollections of everyday life in his youth. This serves as an invitation to provide his audience with the "human side" of life three-quarters of a century ago. The recollection is often penetrated with a running narrative by the person being interviewed of "I remember when . . .," referring to and personally describing events usually noted only in historical documents for most of the audience witnessing the interview. Last, what is typical of such interviews is a request for the respondent to divulge the secret of his longevity. Answers to this question are often prescriptions to maintain good health by abstaining from indulging in such "evils" as smoke and drink, by periodically eating allegedly health-maintaining foodstuffs, or to daily practice a variety of physical-sustenance activities.

The golden image of health which is exalted in interviews with persons of extreme old age again is voluntaristic in that it provides "evidence" that good health may be sustained by simply heeding the prescriptions of persons who have experienced longevity. This portrayal infers that golden health in old age is available to everyone. The image is one of maintaining youthfulness well into life, implying that "you too" can make this choice. It ignores the genetics of longevity, the often structured inaccessibility of persons to sources of health care, and general environmental influences on health sustenance.

Images of Life Satisfaction

Running through the golden images of the social environment of the elderly, their social interaction, and the golden portrayal of health and solvency is a facile and felicitous conception of life satisfaction. The development of life satisfaction is portrayed as a simple function of *voluntaristically* adjusting to "age-appropriate" behavior. The process is conceived as highly individualistic and is not influenced by the potential limitations of either the individual resources or social context of a person's environment.

The golden years myth conceives of aging persons as voluntaristically lowering a variety of social expectations. In a sheer chronological fashion, the aging are said to begin feeling that they need the satisfaction of fewer social events and relationships. Their expectations of entertainment, friendship, and social support in general are said to diminish. As one often hears, elderly persons "like to be alone." They are said to be satisfied with a "busy, but socially uninvolved everyday life."

The desires of the elderly couple are portrayed as socially undemanding. Although they are characterized as ideally busy and self-entertained, they are said to be satisfied with a relatively low degree of outside friendship and other forms of social relationship. Rather, their desires are to "renew their own acquaintance" and to "mutually enrich their own lives." The elderly couple is considered unassuming and undemanding.

The golden image of life satisfaction intensely avoids the problems of social isolation and the need for social support in old age. It conceives of old people as "mature," unselfish persons. Presumably, such aged persons are "beyond the point" of demanding returns on various kinds of social investments. Within those social relationships that exist between the elderly and others, social demands (if any) are not portrayed as having a source in the older person. Any demands that may exist are unilateral, being demands only on the elderly. The older person has no need for discussing everyday problems, for confiding in someone, for seeking the comfort of others in a time of depression, and so forth. Rather, aged persons are considered sources of comfort and confidence for others, especially the young. The image of life satisfaction, then, holds that, upon growing old in years, persons successfully develop into "mature," psychologically self-reliant, and socially independent individuals.

The adjustment of old people to a life of undemanding social relationships and generally limited desires is conceived as being relatively facile. One is said to ideally "grow old gracefully." Images of adjustment problems are rare in the golden years myth. Diminishing desires are a "normal" aspect of aging and considered to be unstormy and rather "noble." The image of facile adjustment portrays aged persons as eager adherents of a conception of unassuming maturity. Aged persons who are disgruntled, who desire the confidence of others, or who are dissatisfied with a growing isolation are considered unadjusted, without allowances being made for differences in the social demands placed on them in various contexts of their everyday lives. Adjustment in the golden years myth is conceived in a very narrow manner. It means commitment to and participation in *one* fairly well defined style of life, the life of a "mature," independently active, and undemanding person. The life satisfaction that is said to emerge from this kind of adjustment is easily attained since it is desired by aged persons who allegedly simply "put it into practice."

Summary of the Myth

On the whole, the various images of the golden years as popularly portrayed and practiced in a variety of public places are images of felicity. Old age is conceived as a normally and generally desirable stage of the life cycle. This normality and desirability are thought of as being a simple function of chronology. The myth leaves little room for differences in styles of aging that are contingent on a variety of social and individual factors.

The popular images of the golden years myth may be summarized as follows:

1. The social environment of old people is conceived as stable and undemanding.
2. The ideal social relationship is portrayed in an image of the "mutually enriching" elderly couple.
3. Older persons are considered highly altruistic, especially in intergenerational relationships.
4. Aging is a process of diminishing needs and desires.
5. Good health is considered to be an outcome of voluntarily being "spry" and "living a healthy life."
6. Life satisfaction is a general and normal response to aging, being a result of persons adjusting themselves to old age.

CRITICISM OF THE MYTH

If there have appeared to be some near or actual contradictions in the foregoing discussion of various aspects of the myth of the golden years, it is because the public portrayal of the golden years is contradictory. The myth is not as much a systematic collection of stereotyped beliefs as it is a body of convenient images. The variety of images is utilized to justify a host of different practices. It is also used to dismiss what could become new kinds of practices. The myth, then, because it is generally used as a convenient justification for dismissing old age rather than as a basis for action on its behalf, has become a set of apologies and rationales. It is in the nature of rationales that serve those who have little interest in concerted change and who would rather dismiss issues (or at least only have "parlor interest" in them) to be glib, gross, and contradictory. There is no social pressure to defend or systematize such a body of beliefs. Because, at present, there is no popular, organized old age movement, the myth of the golden years will continue (1) to be popularly expressed, (2) to be a collection of near contradictory images, and (3) to be a set of rather trivial conceptions popularly held and utilized to dismiss and/or to suppress any active involvement with or challenge to the problems and issues of old age.

If a popular politics of age should emerge, significant changes in the myth of the golden years would take place. The use of various images of the myth would become a more delicate matter than it is now. It would be more difficult to voice glibly a variety of clichés about the aged, to be amused by them, to patronize them, or to readily dismiss them. Such difficulties arise whenever constant and serious challenges emerge to a set of ideas and practices, when the latter are not completely repressive.

To some extent, in the above discussion of the major dimensions of the myth of the golden years, criticism has been evident. In outlining aspects of the myth, references were made to such characteristics as its simplicity and flippancy. In addition to this kind of criticism, however, the myth may be addressed in at least two other ways. One may approach the images from another specific point of view, in our case, the socio-environmental viewpoint. A second approach would contrast what is known empirically about the behavior of old people with various aspects of the myth. Both of these are used in combination below.

Criticism of Social Environment Images

The golden image of the old neighborhood fails to consider the contemporary urban ecology of age-groups. The image portrays the urban social contexts of the aged as neighborhoods of single homes which are stable, community-like, and serviced by local businesses. The distribution of the elderly in urban areas and the characteristics of some of these areas indicate that this image is grossly misleading. The reason why the image is misleading is that it fails to take into consideration the harsh facts of urban neighborhood change in American cities. Given that many neighborhoods have undergone population transition and continue to experience it, what may be said about the question of who it is that moves and who does not as it relates to the aged?

The question of who moves and who does not may be approached in at least two ways in terms of measurement. First, it may be approached subjectively through questions addressed to residents on moving intentions. Second, it may be approached through an objective analysis of the social characteristics of residents, distinguishing those persons who have the resources available to make a move from those persons whose resources are such that making a move would be difficult.

The first of these two approaches has not been an entirely satisfactory predictor of moving in once-relatively-stable (low mobility) neighborhoods. In any stage of neighborhood transition, persons remain who had intentions of moving, and persons move who had intentions of staying (cf. Wolf and Lebeaux, 1969). The resources of those who actually move and those who actually stay in a transition neighborhood are related to moving. The analysis of residents' resources shows that those persons who do remain in transition neighborhoods, but who wish to move, are often those whose resources are relatively poor. Thus, one answer to the question of who moves and who remains in changing neighborhoods is that those who can least afford to move stay behind.

If the resources of the aged are examined, they as a group fall heavily into the category of residents least able to afford a move. This is so for several reasons: (1) their incomes are comparatively low, (2) they are likely to have made relatively extensive investments in their neighborhoods, and (3) they are less physiologically able to cope with the problems of physical movement. It should not be surprising, then, that when older neighborhoods or neighborhoods that have undergone extensive population transition are examined, those persons who are "long-time" residents and are the remnants of an earlier neighborhood composition are often the aged.

In view of this, the golden image of "grandmother's house" is rather dubious. Although it may be a bit of nostalgia and may continue to exist in some places, it certainly is not an appropriate description of the general urban social environment of old people. If anything, an overall portrait of the social conditions of the urban neighborhoods of old people would have to include cases of relative neighborhood isolation, increasing rates of local crime, and fear.

There is another problem with the image of the urban social contexts of the aged. It is too narrow. Aside from the fact that the image of single home, urban neighborhoods does not consider the impact of transition on aged persons remaining in them, the image is too limited in its portrayal of the kinds of urban social contexts in which the aged reside. A significant number of aged persons rent their housing in urban areas. They reside in hotels, boarding homes, apartments, and rented rooms. These persons are fairly well hidden from a variety of available services because (1) their residences are not often publicly known as housing the aged, which (2) makes it unlikely that age-related services will seek them out, and (3) the information on available services is not likely to reach them since there are usually no formally established means of systematic contact. Such "hidden" old people themselves often are not aware of age-related facilities so that they, on their own, do not take the initiative in finding them (cf. Ossofsky, 1970).

This criticism of the golden image of an old person's neighborhood is not intended to give the impression that all urban neighborhoods in which the aged reside are crime-ridden and unstable. Rather, what is intended is noting that the conditions of the social environments of old people in urban areas are not necessarily aligned with the characteristics of the myth. There are many kinds of local social contexts in urban areas in which the aged reside. However, because of the state of their resources in general, the elderly as a group are likely to be disproportionately represented in areas which are quite a contrast from that portrayed in the myth.

The golden image of social contexts includes the retirement community and the convalescent home. They are characterized as trouble-free, felicitous, and "available to you!" Again, this image is too simple in that it does not take into consideration the state of the resources of old people.

Although it certainly may be true that retirement communities do offer aged persons a variety of activities and the potential for developing extensive friendships, it is by no means the case that they are available to an old person "for the asking." If anything, such communities are within the financial accessibility of only a small proportion of the aged. It is not true that old people can simply take the initiative "to build a new life for themselves and enjoy the retirement years." The fact is that, regardless of intentions, there are strong limitations to the mobility of the aged, not the least of which is solvency.

The golden image also extends to the convalescent center.

This image, like the preceding one, is extensively propagated through the literature and spokesmen advertising it. The image is questionable in two ways. First, the availability of this kind of facility to the aged is limited in the same way as in the retirement community. It is beyond the financial capability of many old people, for the cost of "convalescence" in these facilities is generally high. Second, the image of "total care" propagated by convalescent facilities is not wholly accurate. In recent years, the inadequacies of many nursing home facilities have been the subject of extensive hearings. These hearings, which are being initiated in one state after another, have led to the gradual realization of the need for much greater regulation than now exists (cf. United States Senate, Special Committee on Aging, 1970, pp. 80-90).

What runs through popular images of each of these social contexts is the idea that they place few, if any, burdens on old people. Once in them, the aged allegedly either lead rich domestic lives, enjoy their retirement years, or experience the "tender and full care of a concerned" facility. The myth of the golden years shows no concern for variations in environmental demands and constraints on the elderly.

Criticism of Social Interaction Images

One of the most popular images of the golden years myth is that of the mutually enriched elderly couple. It is implicitly claimed that the greatest degree of life satisfaction in old age is an outcome of a "chance to enjoy each other's company in the sunset years." Again, as with other aspects of the myth, the hypothesis that life satisfaction is an outcome of having a living spouse in old age is too simple.

The problem with the image of the elderly couple is that it ignores social constraints on the lives of aged persons. It assumes that persons are individuals, that such persons do have complete control over their lives, and that such control is rationally manipulated to gain various ends. The golden years myth omits salient features of social life and their impact on persons—such facts as public expectations on behavior which

may vary from one situation to another, physical constra... on ior
the everyday life of the aged, and the differences in behav
facilitation that various social contexts provide.

There are, in fact, several kinds of "rich" old age. The ideal
kind of social life in old age is not limited to the elderly couple.
Life satisfaction may exist in various social contexts, depending
on the relationship between the characteristics of the contexts,
on the one hand, and the individual characteristics of persons,
on the other.

Blau (1961), among others, has shown evidence of how
simple the golden image of social interaction in fact is. In a
study of the life satisfaction of widows in relation to their ability
to make friends, she notes that it is not the case that simple
widowhood leads persons to be, as several women in the Detroit
Study mentioned, "fifth wheels." Blau indicates that the social
isolation of widows is an outcome of being in social contexts in
which the majority of persons have living spouses. In contrast
to this, widows in a context with other widows tend not to be
isolated, leading comparatively "rich" and satisfied lives with
strong, relatively extensive friendships. In these widowed social
contexts, it is likely to be the elderly married couple that feels
socially isolated.

The portrayal of the widow, and especially the widower, as
somewhat deviant in the golden image of social interaction is
inaccurate. The deviant image is primarily one of an isolated,
brooding, and rather eccentric old man. Blau's evidence, as well
as much observation of spouseless aged men in the Detroit
Study, indicate that this may occur frequently in one type of
social context only, namely, when such persons do not have
access readily to similarly situated others.

In the Detroit Study, it was quite apparent that in those
social contexts where widowers were relatively visible and the
chances of their encountering each other were comparatively
high, they were likely to become well integrated into a peer
group. It was not unusual to find a collection of such persons
gathering routinely at a particular time and place to "talk things
over," or to simply sit together and "watch" things. Rather close

ships developed out of such routines. Because these persons
re all single or widowed men, their initial encounters occurred
with a rather common underpinning in their lives. This facilitates
social interaction. In Detroit, it was obvious that such men came
to look forward to the routine conviviality of friends and were
well satisfied with their daily participation in the life of "the
boys."

The routines of widowed men that gathered, sat, and watched
in Detroit, were at times highly convivial and at other times
appeared to be what might be referred to simply as "watches."
Their conviviality typically was a kind of amused bantering.
There was extensive cajoling in these exchanges with a great
deal of laughter. The men would be highly taken with the
success of one of them at "pulling someone's leg." The practice
of watching was quite different from the bantering. For one
thing, it was rather silent with occasional unclear expressions
of judgment being heard about a passing event. This watching
tends to focus on some occurrence within sight. It involves
peering rather intently at the "unusual," e.g. at a person vividly
dressed, at a woman with exceptionally large breasts, or at a
construction or demolition site. Any unusual event easily becomes
the subject of discussion in the next gathering.

A second image of social interaction among the aged portrays
life satisfaction as high when interaction is intergenerational.
This image of intergenerational interaction also has its more professional side. For example, it is at the center of the debate
over whether social integration into mixed-age (age-heterogeneous) community life is more or less demoralizing to aged
persons than segregation from such community life. Although
this debate continues, there is mounting evidence that intergenerational encounters are not as likely to lead to friendship,
to be as satisfying, and to make for the social integration of the
elderly as are intragenerational encounters. Much of this evidence, which was discussed earlier in this book (see Chap. III),
comes from studies of variations in friendship and life satisfaction
associated with social contexts with differing degrees of age-
homogeneity.

A third golden image of social interaction portrays life satisfaction as emerging from a "busy" life. The image frowns on idleness. It associates life satisfaction with clubbing, having hobbies, or game-like activity; the portrayal is one of old persons exuberantly "involved." This image is at variance with the sometimes expressed desire of aged persons to "simply sit together and quietly enjoy our company like anyone else." It certainly is at variance with the practice of "watching," which was played with great self-confessed satisfaction by older men interviewed and observed in Detroit.

The myth does not distinguish possible contextual variations in social expectations. Different groups of persons may define life satisfaction in radically different ways. If the social life in one context is typified by active involvement in a variety of activities and/or work, the elderly within it should (given that they are oriented to it) feel dissatisfied if they are idle or unable to maintain the same degree of activeness and involvement. On the other hand, if one's social context is built around norms of relative inactivity in everyday life, dissatisfaction is more likely to be a function of too great a desire for "involvement." Here, it is idle persons, by choice or necessity, who should maintain fairly high morale.

One aspect of the golden myth of old age that appears in several portrayals of social interaction is that of retirement planning. It exists in a host of popular slogans about and solutions for "successful aging." Planning for retirement is part of the voluntaristic character of the myth of the golden years.

Studies of retirement planning and the outcomes of such planning indicate that planning per se is not necessarily a safeguard against life dissatisfaction in the post-retirement period of persons' lives. In 1958, Wayne E. Thompson published the results of a study of the impact of preretirement planning on adjustment in retirement. The focus of the study was on whether, in fact, planning for the kind of social life that one will have upon retirement results in better adjustment than not planning. Thompson's data provide evidence that the golden maxims of "make something of your life," and "build a satisfying later life" are too simple as descriptions of the social life that persons may expect in old age after retirement.

Thompson's study used a panel design which consisted of interviews with the same working individuals both before and after retirement. The year preceding retirement, respondents were asked questions about three factors which could significantly affect adjustment in retirement. Indexes measuring (1) attitude toward retirement, (2) preconception of retirement life, and (3) plans for retirement, were administered to the panel of respondents. A year after retirement, the following three factors were tapped: (1) length of time to adjust, (2) difficulty in keeping busy, and (3) dissatisfaction with retirement.

The findings indicate that each of the three preretirement factors just mentioned has some independent impact on adjustment after retirement when adjustment is measured by the length of time respondents report that it took them to get used to not working. The important result of the study in terms of the qualification it presents for the golden image of planning is the interrelationship of planning, on the one hand, and accuracy of conception of retirement, on the other, as it affects postretirement adjustment. Among persons who did not have an accurate conception of what retirement would be like, those who had made retirement plans *more frequently* took longer than three months to become used to not working than those who hadn't made any plans. In these instances, planning was *more* detrimental to post-retirement adjustment than not planning at all.

When Thompson's finding on the impact of planning on postretirement adjustment is contrasted with the golden portrayal of retirement planning, one resulting conclusion is that the golden image of retirement may perpetuate difficult postretirement adjustment for some persons. Those workers nearing retirement age who (1) make retirement plans, (2) base their conception of retirement on information provided by golden public images, and (3) whose preretirement resources indicate that retirement may mean a severe curtailment of a variety of activities, are likely to have a difficult postretirement adjustment.

If the varied images of old age and retirement that are

portrayed by the golden years myth are considered sources of information, then for some older workers, images are the only indication which they have of what they can expect of their lives when they end their full-time working careers. For some of these workers, who have no source of counter-information, retirement planning is likely to be a more self-defeating effort than not planning at all. Because public images do serve as sources of information for persons nearing retirement, it is evident that some form of preretirement education is necessary to inform these individuals of the potential problems and conditions of post-retirement life styles. In recent years, educators have indeed become aware of this problem and efforts have been undertaken, primarily through the larger corporations, to institute preretirement educational programs of various sorts.

Criticism of Solvency and Health Images

The golden image of solvency in old age is linked to a conception of declining needs. As persons age, the monies or monetary equivalents that it requires to fulfill everyday needs are said to decline. Consequently, existing income maintenance programs are considered adequate for the elderly. The problem with this conception of declining needs is that needs are defined in terms of active, working adults and extrapolated onto later life. It fails to consider the possibility that new kinds of needs emerge as a result of qualitative alterations in everyday living that come with growing old in the United States.

Aside from a very basic financial need that is a function of having low incomes, the aged have other monetary needs that result from physiological aging per se. These other needs place a heavy burden on the adequacy of basic income. They fall into two major categories: the financial assistance needed for (1) medical attention that is required by declining health, and (2) services to replace those provided by a spouse or other individual before death.

Declining health has an equivalence in loss of income. Low cost services of which a person may take advantage if he is in minimally good health become unavailable to those in poor health. Services which fulfill the same functions for the healthy as for the unhealthy cost the latter more than they do persons in good health. Those who can least afford it suffer the most in terms of rising costs due to health. Take the matter of transportation. Public transportation, which is minimal in cost to the user in comparison with other forms of transit, becomes unavailable to some of the aged because, compared to other forms of transit, it assumes a higher degree of activeness and physical ability in riders. For instance, it takes more energy and effort to walk to, wait for, board, and descend a bus than it does to be transported by automobile to some destination. Low cost transit also has a variety of other age-linked burdens associated with it, e.g. the comparative inability of the aged to deal with exiting crowded vehicles, or their vulnerability to being criminally victimized while in transit. Those persons who cannot take advantage of low-cost transit because of poor mobility skills must either pay more for alternate transit services or do without them.

Solvency problems may emerge also from loss of the income equivalent provided by a living spouse. This is likely to increase the monetary needs of the elderly as a group in a way that is not typical of younger age-groups. For example, an elderly female may have depended on her spouse for a variety of daily services which he contributed to the household. He might have repaired gadgets or other things himself. He might have transported himself and his wife to local facilities and conveniences. For an elderly male, his wife may have been a source of hot meals, comfort, and other daily necessities. In short, a married couple, over time, divide their labors between a variety of services to each other which satisfy many everyday needs, some minor and others which are quite important. In the division of such labors, each becomes dependent on the other for provisions contributed toward their common welfare. This dependence, however, also means that each loses a certain amount of ability to be independent of the other. The problem makes the death of a spouse especially difficult for an elderly person. First, there is the loss of a variety of services, and second, companionship. Third, what may be a more difficult problem to deal with is the fact that a person has lost the income equivalent of such services. He or she now more likely has to pay for them, e.g. being transported by automobile or eating hot meals.

As far as the golden image of health per se is concerned, what runs through both the public portrayal of spryness and the exaltation of extreme old age is the theme that (1) both of these conditions are goals for the elderly and (2) they may be gained through individual effort. Again, as at other points of the myth of the golden years, the assumption of voluntarism is evident. What the image of health suggests is that it is the mere decision to live a long and healthy life, on the one hand, and long-term planning for this, on the other, that makes for both spryness and longevity. As the image of health is portrayed, the proof of this lies in the testament of persons who are visibly spry and have lived into extreme old age. Needless to say, this kind of argument always wins its case.

Criticism of the Image of Life Satisfaction

The image of life satisfaction is built on a single conception of adjustment. To be adjusted in old age, it is implied, is to exhibit the following behavior: (1) above all, to be "happy," (2) to be altruistically involved with younger persons, (3) to maintain a "busy" everyday life, and (4) to accept voluntarily the comparatively deprived social conditions that exist for many aged persons. As should be obvious, adjustment is defined primarily in terms of compliance with the ongoing social conditions of being old in America. When an aged person accepts and commits himself to the status quo, and is happy with his acceptance, he is considered to have adjusted to old age. Life satisfaction is said to follow adjustment.

A central issue in the foregoing approach to adjustment is that it is a basically conservative idea and thus is not, by any means, the only way to define it. It certainly may be thought of as *one* particular approach to a definition. However, other less conservative approaches are conceivable.

All conceptions of adjustment, explicit or not, conservative or otherwise, focus on the relationship between two things:

(1) the behavior of persons, and (2) the social conditions of everyday life. The *conservative* approach to adjustment, on which the golden image of life satisfaction is founded, does not question the desirability of social conditions but rather concerns itself with the adaptation or adjustment of personal behavior to these conditions. The key to adjustment, from the conservative point of view, lies in the acceptance of and felicitous commitment of persons to these conditions. Ideal adjustment, then, becomes a state of altruistic involvement with the current circumstances of everyday life in old age. What might be called the *radical* approach to adjustment assumes that social conditions are dispensible and are tolerated only as far as they contribute to human well-being. Consequently, when social conditions perpetuate misery, persons are defined as unadjusted if they accept and altruistically commit themselves to them. A kind of "ideal unadjustment" emerges, from the radical point of view, when persons are found fully committed to social conditions which they are unaware perpetuate their feelings of extreme uneasiness and anxiety in everyday life.

In view of its political undercurrents, the golden image of adjustment (as with other approaches to this concept) is an ideology. Its image of life satisfaction, being tied to the adjustment of persons to ongoing conditions of social life, perpetuates the acceptance of growing old as it currently occurs. It is not a general conception of adjustment in old age but rather one approach to it.

One final thing should be noted. Although the foregoing discussion tended to emphasize some of the more negative contingencies of aging in America, it should not be concluded that old age is, by necessity, a period of want, social isolation, and life dissatisfaction. The intention of this discussion has been to indicate (1) that old age is a period characterized by these conditions for a significant number of elderly persons, (2) that old age is not always "golden" although it may be in some cases, and (3) that more factors than individual decision-making and getting chronologically older influence the outcome of aging.

REFERENCES

Albrecht, Ruth: Social roles of old people. *Journal of Gerontology*, 6:138-145, 1951.

Aldridge, Gordon J.: Informal social relationships in a retirement community. *Marriage and Family Living*, 21:70-72, 1959.

Allport, Gordon W.: *The Nature of Prejudice*. Garden City, N.Y., Doubleday & Company, 1958.

Barron, Milton L.: Minority group characteristics of the aged in American society. *Journal of Gerontology*, 8:477-481, 1953.

Becker, Howard S.: *Outsiders*. New York, The Free Press, 1963.

Bekker, L. D., and Taylor, C.: Attitudes toward the aged in a multigenerational sample. *Journal of Gerontology*, 21:115-118, 1966.

Bengston, Vern L.: Inter-age perceptions and the generation gap. *The Gerontologist*, 11:85-89, 1971.

Berelson, B. R., Lazarsfeld, P. F., and McPhee, W. N.: *Voting*. Chicago, University of Chicago Press, 1954.

Berger, Peter L., and Luckmann, Thomas: *The Social Construction of Reality*. Garden City, N.Y., Doubleday & Company, 1966.

Beyer, Glenn H., and Wahl, Sylvia G.: *The Elderly and Their Housing*. Ithaca, N.Y., Cornell University Agricultural Experiment Station, 1963.

Beyer, Glenn H., and Woods, Margaret E.: Living and activity patterns of the aged. Research Report No. 6, Ithaca, N.Y., Center for Housing and Environmental Studies, Cornell University, 1963.

Blau, Peter M.: *Exchange and Power in Social Life*. New York, Wiley, 1964.

Blau, Zena Smith: Changes in status and age identification. *American Sociological Review*, 21:198-203, 1956.

Blau, Zena Smith: Structural constraints on friendship in old age. *American Sociological Review*, 26:429-439, 1961.

Blumer, Herbert: *Symbolic Interaction*. Englewood Cliffs, N.J., Prentice-Hall, 1969.

Bultena, Gordon L., and Marshall, Douglas G.: Structural effects on the morale of the aged: a comparative analysis of age-segregated and age-integrated communities. Paper presented at the annual meeting of the American Sociological Association, San Francisco, 1969.

Bultena, Gordon L., and Wood, Vivian: The American retirement community: bane or blessing? Paper presented at the annual meeting of the Gerontological Society, Denver, 1968.

Campbell, Ernest, and Alexander, Norman: Structural effects and interpersonal relationships. *American Journal of Sociology*, 71:284-289, 1965.

Caplow, Theodore, and Forman, Robert: Neighborhood interaction in a homogeneous community. *American Sociological Review*, 15:357-366, 1950.

Carp, Frances M.: The impact of environment on old people. *The Gerontologist*, 7:106-108, 1967.

Carp, Frances M.: Walking as a means of transportation for retired people. *The Gerontologist*, 11:104-111, 1971.

Cavan, Ruth S.: Self and role in adjustment during old age. In Rose, Arnold M. (Ed.): *Human Behavior and Social Processes*. Boston, Houghton Mifflin, 1962, pp. 526-536.

Cavan, Ruth S., Burgess, Ernest W., Havighurst, Robert J., and Goldhammer, Herbert: *Personal Adjustment in Old Age*. Chicago, Science Research Associates, 1949.

Cooley, Charles Horton: *Human Nature and the Social Order*. New York, Shocken Books, 1964.

Cumming, Elaine: Further thoughts on the theory of disengagement. *International Social Science Journal*, 15:377-393, 1963.

Cumming, Elaine, Dean, Lois R., Newell, David S., and McCaffrey, Isabel: Disengagement—a tentative theory of aging. *Sociometry*, 23:23-35, 1960.

Cumming, Elaine, and Henry, William E.: *Growing Old*. New York, Basic Books, 1961.

Dreitzel, Hans Peter (Ed.): *Recent Sociology No. 2*. New York, Macmillan, 1970.

Ennis, Philip H.: *Criminal Victimization in the United States*. Chicago, National Opinion Research Center, University of Chicago, 1967.

Etzioni, Amitai: The epigenesis of political communities at the international level. *American Journal of Sociology*, 68:407-421, 1963.

Festinger, Leon: *A Theory of Cognitive Dissonance*. Stanford, Calif., Stanford University Press, 1957.

Festinger, Leon, Riecken, Henry W., and Schachter, Stanley: *When Prophecy Fails*. New York, Harper & Row, 1956.

Festinger, Leon, Schachter, Stanley, and Back, Kurt: *Social Pressures in Informal Groups*. New York, Harper & Brothers, 1950.

Fishbein, Martin: Attitude and the prediction of behavior. In Fishbein, Martin (Ed.): *Readings in Attitude Theory and Research*, New York, Wiley, 1967, pp. 477-492.

Fisher, Lloyd H.: Research in the politics of age. In Donahue, Wilma, and Tibbitts, Clark (Eds.): *Politics of Age*. Ann Arbor, Mich., University of Michigan, Division of Gerontology, 1962, pp. 36-47.

Friedrichs, Robert W.: *A Sociology of Sociology*. New York, The Free Press, 1970.

Gans, Herbert J.: Planning and social life. *Journal of the American Institute of Planners*, 27:134-140, 1961.

Garfinkel, Harold: *Studies in Ethnomethodology*. Englewood Cliffs, N.J., Prentice-Hall, 1967.

Gersuny, Carl: The rhetoric of the retirement home industry. *The Gerontologist*, 10:282-286, 1970.

Gerth, Hans, and Mills, C. Wright: *Character and Social Structure.* New York, Harcourt, Brace & World, 1953.

Glaser, Barney G., and Strauss, Anselm: *The Discovery of Grounded Theory.* Chicago, Aldine, 1967.

Goffman, Erving: *Asylums.* Garden City, N.Y., Doubleday & Company, 1961.

Goffman, Erving: *The Presentation of Self in Everyday Life.* Garden City, N.Y., Doubleday & Company, 1959.

Gubrium, Jaber F.: Continuity in social support, political interest, and voting in old age. *The Gerontologist, 12:*421-423, 1972.

Gubrium, Jaber F.: Environmental effects on morale in old age and the resources of health and solvency. *The Gerontologist, 10:*294-297, 1970.

Gubrium, Jaber F.: Self-conceptions of mental health among the aged. *Mental Hygiene, 55:*398-403, 1971.

Hamovitch, Maurice: Social and psychological factors in adjustment in a retirement village. In Carp, Frances (Ed.): *The Retirement Process.* Washington, Public Health Service, U.S. Department of Health, Education, and Welfare, 1966, pp. 115-125.

Harding, John; Kutner, Bernard, Proshansky, Harold, and Chein, Isidor: Prejudice and ethnic relations. In Lindzey, Gardner (Ed.): *Handbook of Social Psychology,* Reading, Mass., 1954.

Havighurst, Robert J., and Albrecht, Ruth: *Older People.* New York, Longmans, 1953.

Heider, Fritz: Attitudes and cognitive organization. *Journal of Psychology. 21:*107-112, 1946.

Henry, William E.: Engagement and disengagement: toward a theory of adult development. In Kastenbaum, Robert (Ed.): *Contributions To The Psychobiology of Aging.* New York, Springer, 1965, pp. 19-35.

Heyman, Dorothy K., and Jeffers, Frances C.: Effect of time lapse on consistency of self-health and medical evaluations of elderly persons. *Journal of Gerontology, 18:*160-164, 1963.

Homans, George C.: *Social Behavior: Its Elementary Forms.* New York, Harcourt, Brace & World, 1961.

Hunter, Woodrow W., and Maurice, Helen: *Older People Tell Their Story.* Ann Arbor, Mich., Institute for Human Adjustment, Division of Gerontology, 1953.

Hutchinson, Bertram: *Old People in a Modern Australian Community.* New York, Cambridge University Press, 1954.

Kogan, N.: Attitudes toward old people: the development of a scale and an examination of correlates. *Journal of Abnormal and Social Psychology, 62:*44-54, 1961.

Kogan, N., and Wallach, Michael A.: Age changes in values and attitudes. *Journal of Gerontology, 16:*272-280, 1961.

Kossoris, Max: Absenteeism and injury experience of older workers. *Monthly Labor Review, 67:*16-19, 1948.

Kuhn, Thomas S.: *The Structure of Scientific Revolutions*. Chicago, University of Chicago, 1962.

Kutner, Bernard, Fanshel, David, Togo, Alice M., and Langner, Thomas S.: *Five Hundred Over Sixty*. New York, Russell Sage, 1956.

Langford, Marilyn: Community aspects of housing for the aged. Research report No. 5, Ithaca, N.Y., Center for Housing and Environmental Studies, Cornell University, 1962.

Lemert, Edwin: Paranoia and the dynamics of exclusion. *Sociometry,* 25:2-20, 1962.

Lockwood, David: Some remarks on 'The Social System.' In Demerath III, N. J., and Peterson, Richard A. (Eds.): *System, Change, and Conflict.* New York, The Free Press, 1967, pp. 281-291.

Lowenthal, Marjorie Fiske: Social isolation and mental illness in old age. *American Sociological Review,* 29:54-70, 1964.

Maccoby, Herbert: The differential political activity of participants in a voluntary association. *American Sociological Review,* 23:524-532, 1958.

Maddox, George L.: Activity and morale: a longitudinal study of selected elderly subjects. *Social Forces, 42:*195-204, 1963.

Maddox, George L.: Disengagement theory: a critical evaluation. *The Gerontologist, 4:*80-82, 1964.

Maddox, George L.: Face and artifact: evidence bearing on disengagement theory from the Duke Geriatric Project. *Human Development, 8:*117-130, 1965.

Maddox, George L.: A longitudinal multidisciplinary study of human aging: selected methodological issues. *Proceedings of the Social Statistics Section,* American Statistical Association, 280-285, 1962a.

Maddox, George L.: Some correlates of differences in self-assessment of health status among the elderly. *Journal of Gerontology, 17:*180-185, 1962b.

Maddox, George L.: Persistence of life style among the elderly: a longitudinal study of patterns of social activity in relation to life satisfaction. *Proceedings, 7th International Congress of Gerontology,* Vienna, 6:309-311, 1966.

Maddox, George L.: Themes and issues in sociological theories of human aging. *Human Development, 13:*17-27, 1970.

Maddox, George L., and Eisdorfer, Carl: Some correlates of activity and morale among the elderly. *Social Forces, 40:*254, 260, 1962.

Malinowski, Bronislaw: Anthropology. In *Encyclopaedia Britannica,* First supplementary volume, London and New York, 1926, pp. 132-133.

Markovitz, Joni K.: Transportation needs of the elderly. *Traffic Quarterly,* 25:237-253, 1971.

Marshall, Douglas G.: Migration and old people in a rural community: the story of Price County, Wisconsin. In Rose, Arnold M., and Peterson, Warren A. (Eds.): *Older People and Their Social World.* Philadelphia, F. A. Davis, 1965, pp. 341-355.

Maves, Paul B.: Aging, religion and the church. In Tibbits, Clark (Ed.): *Handbook of Social Gerontology.* Chicago, University of Chicago Press, 1960, pp. 698-749.

McTavish, Donald G.: Perceptions of old people: a review of research methodologies and findings. *The Gerontologist, 11*:90-101, 1971.

Mead, George H.: *Mind, Self, and Society.* Chicago, University of Chicago Press, 1934.

Merrill, S. E., and Gunter, L. M.: A study of patient attitudes toward old people. *Geriatrics, 24*:107-112, 1969.

Merton, Robert K.: *Social Theory and Social Structure.* New York, The Free Press, 1957.

Merton, Robert K., and Lazarsfeld, Paul: Friendship as a social process. In Berger, Morroe, Abel, Theodore, and Page, Charles (Eds.): *Freedom and Control in Modern Society.* Princeton, N.J., Van Nostrand, 1954, pp. 18-66.

Messer, Mark, The possibility of an age-concentrated environment becoming a normative system. *The Gerontologist, 7*:247-250, 1967.

Milner, K. O.: The environment as a factor in the etiology of criminal paranoia. *Journal of Mental Science, 95*:124-132, 1949.

Neugarten, Bernice L.: Personality and patterns of aging. Paper presented at the meeting of the Dutch Gerontological Society, 1965.

Neugarten, Bernice L., Havighurst, Robert J., and Tobin, Sheldon S.: The measurement of life satisfaction. *Journal of Gerontology, 16*:134-143, 1961.

Neugarten, Bernice L., and Peterson, W. A.: A study of the American age-grade system. *Proceedings, 4th Congress of the International Association of Gerontology, Bolzano, Italy, 1-6, 1957.*

Newcomb, Theodore M.: An approach to the study of communicative acts. *Psychological Review, 60*:393-404, 1953.

Osgood, Charles E., and Tannenbaum, Percy H.: The principle of congruity in the prediction of attitude change. *Psychological Review, 62*:42-55, 1955.

Ossofsky, Jack: *The Golden Years: A Tarnished Myth, The Project FIND Report.* New York, The National Council on Aging, 1970.

Palmore, Erdman: Retirement patterns among aged men: findings of the 1963 survey of the aged. *Social Security Bulletin, 27*:3-10, August, 1964.

Palmore, Erdman: Sociological aspects of aging. In Busse, Ewald W., and Pfeiffer, Eric (Eds.): *Behavior and Adaptation in Late Life.* Boston, Litte, Brown, 1969, pp. 33-69.

Palmore, Erdman, and Whittington, Frank: Trends in the relative status of the aged. *Social Forces, 50*:84-91, 1971.

Parsons, Talcott: *The Social System.* New York, The Free Press, 1951.

Parsons, Talcott, and Shils, Edward A. (Eds.): *Toward a General Theory of Action.* New York, Harper & Row, 1951.

Pederson, S.: Psychological reactions to social displacement (refugee neurosis). *Psychoanalytic Review*, 36:344-354, 1946.

Phillips, Bernard S.: A role theory approach to adjustment in old age. *American Sociological Review*, 22:212-217, 1957.

Pihlblad, C. Terence, and McNamara, Robert L.: Social adjustment of elderly people in three small towns. In Rose, Arnold M., and Peterson, Warren A. (Eds.): *Older People and Their Social World*. Philadelphia, F. A. Davis, 1965, pp. 49-73.

Pinner, Frank A., Jacobs, Paul, and Selznick, Philip: *Old Age and Political Behavior*. Berkeley, University of California Press, 1959.

Popper, Karl R.: *Conjectures and Refutations*. New York, Basic Books, 1965.

Riley, Matilda White, and Foner, Anne: *Aging and Society*. New York, Russell Sage, 1968.

Rose, Arnold M.: A current theoretical issue in social gerontology. *The Gerontologist*, 4:46-50, 1964.

Rose, Arnold M.: Group consciousness among the aging. In Rose, Arnold M., and Peterson, Warren A. (Eds.): *Older People and Their Social World*. Philadelphia, F. A. Davis Company, 1965a, pp. 19-36.

Rose, Arnold M.: Organizations for the elderly: political implications. In Donahue, Wilma, and Tibbitts, Clark (Eds.): *Politics of Age*. Ann Arbor, Mich., University of Michigan, Division of Gerontology, 1962b, pp. 135-145.

Rose, Arnold M.: A social-psychological theory of neurosis. In Rose, Arnold M. (Ed.): *Human Behavior and Social Processes*. Boston, Houghton Mifflin, 1962a, pp. 537-549.

Rose, Arnold M.: The subculture of the aging: a framework for research in social gerontology. In Rose, Arnold M., and Peterson, Warren A. (Eds.): *Older People and Their Social World*. Philadelphia, F. Davis Company, 1965b, pp. 3-16.

Rose, Arnold M., and Peterson, Warren A. (Eds.): *Older People and Their Social World*. Philadelphia, F. A. Davis Company, 1965.

Rosenberg, George S.: *The Worker Grows Old*. San Francisco, Jossey-Bass, 1970.

Rosencranz, H., and McNevin, T.: A factor analysis of attitudes toward the aged. *The Gerontologist*, 9:55-59, 1969.

Rosow, Irving: *Social Integration of the Aged*. New York, The Free Press, 1967.

Scotch, Norman A., and Richardson, Arthur H.: Characteristics of the self-sufficient among the very aged. *Proceedings, 7th International Congress of Gerontology, Vienna*, 8:489-493, 1966.

Secord, P. F., and Backman, C. W.: An interpersonal approach to personality. In Maher, B. (Ed.): *Progress in Experimental Personality Research*. New York, Academic Press, 1965, pp. 91-125.

Secord, P. F., and Backman, C. W.: Personality theory and the problem of stability and change in individual behavior: an interpersonal approach. *Psychological Review, 68*:21-32, 1961.

Shanas, Ethel: *The Health of Older People: A Social Survey.* Cambridge, Harvard University Press, 1962.

Shanas, Ethel, *et al.*: *Old People in Three Industrial Societies.* New York, Atherton Press, 1968.

Scheff, Thomas J.: *Being Mentally Ill.* Chicago, Aldine, 1966.

Shibutani, Tamotsu, and Kwan, Kian M.: *Ethnic Stratification.* New York, Macmillan, 1965.

Simmel, Georg: *Conflict and the Web of Group Affiliations.* Glencoe, Ill., The Free Press, 1955.

Simmel, Georg: *The Sociology of Georg Simmel.* New York, The Free Press, 1950.

Simmons, Leo W.: *The Role of the Aged in Primitive Societies.* New Haven, Yale University Press, 1945.

Srole, Leo: Social integration and certain corollaries. *American Sociological Review, 21*:709-716, 1956.

Strauss, Anselm *et al.*: The hospital and its negotiated order. In Freidson, Eliot (Ed.): *The Hospital in Modern Society.* New York, The Free Press, 1963, pp. 147-169.

Streib, Gordon F.: Are the aged a minority group? In Gouldner, Alvin W., and Miller, S. M. (Eds.): *Applied Sociology.* Glencoe, Ill., The Free Press, 1965a, pp. 311-328.

Streib, Gordon F.: Longitudinal study of retirement. Final Report to the Social Security Administration, Washington, D.C., 1965b.

Streib, Gordon F., and Thompson, W. E.: Personal and social adjustment in retirement. In Donahue, Wilma, and Tibbitts, Clark (Eds.): *The New Frontiers of Aging.* Ann Arbor, Mich., University of Michigan Press, 1957, pp. 180-197.

Suchman, Edward A., Phillips, Bernard S., and Streib, Gordon F.: An analysis of the validity of health questionnaires. *Social Forces, 36*:223-232, 1958.

Taietz, Phillip, and Larson, Olaf F.: Social participation and old age. *Rural Sociology, 21*:229-238, 1956.

Talmon, Garber, Yonina: Aging in collective settlement in Israel. In Tibbitts, Clark and Donahue, Wilma (Eds.): *Social and Psychological Aspects of Aging.* New York, Columbia University Press, 1962, pp. 426-441.

Thompson, Wayne E.: Pre-retirement anticipation and adjustment in retirement. *Journal of Social Issues, 14*:35-45, 1958.

Tobin, Sheldon S., and Neugarten, Bernice L.: Life satisfaction and social interaction in the aging. *Journal of Gerontology, 16*:344-346, 1961.

Townsend, Peter: *The Family Life of Old People.* London, Routledge & Kegan, Paul, 1957.

Townsend, Peter: Isolation, desolation, and loneliness. In Shanas, Ethel, et al.: *Old People in Three Industrial Societies.* New York, Atherton Press, 1968, pp. 258-287.

Trela, James L.: Some political consequences of senior center and other old age group memberships. *The Gerontologist, 11*:118-123, 1971.

Troll, Lillian E., and Schlossberg, Nancy: A preliminary investigation of "age bias" in helping professions. *The Gerontologist, 10*:46, 1970.

Tucker, Charles W.: Some methodological problems of Kuhn's self theory. *The Sociological Quarterly, 7*:345-358, 1966.

Tuckman, J., and Lorge, I.: Attitudes toward old people. *Journal of Social Psychology, 37*:249-260, 1953.

Tuckman, J., and Lorge, I.: Attitudes toward older workers. *Journal of Applied Psychology, 36*:149-153, 1952.

Tunstall, Jeremy: *Old and Alone: A Sociological Study of Old People.* London, Routledge and Kegan Paul, 1966.

United States Bureau of the Census: *Current Population Reports.* P-20, No. 143, Washington, D.C., Government Printing Office, 1965.

United States Senate, Special committee on aging: *Developments in Aging, 1969.* Report No. 91-875, Washington, D.C., Government Printing Office, 1970.

Weber, Max: *The Theory of Social and Economic Organization.* Glencoe, Ill., The Free Press, 1947.

Weiss, Robert S.: The fund of sociability. *Transaction, 6*:36-43, 1969.

Whyte, William H.: *The Organization Man.* New York, Doubleday & Company, 1956.

Wolf, Eleanor P., and Lebeaux, Charles N.: *Change and Renewal in an Urban Community: Five Case Studies of Detroit.* New York, Praeger Publishers, 1969.

INDEX